MW00698650

Essence *of* Buddhism

Essence *of* Buddhism

VENERABLE MASTER HSING YUN

Buddha's Light Publishing

© 2012 Buddha's Light Publishing
First Edition

By Venerable Master Hsing Yun
Translated by FGS Int'l Translation Center
Edited by John Gill
Book Design by Wan Kah Ong

Publishing by Buddha's Light Publishing
3456 S. Glenmark Drive
Hacienda Heights, CA 91745, U.S.A.
Tel: (626) 923-5144   Fax: (626) 923-5145
www.blpusa.com   itc@blia.org

Printed in Taiwan.

CONTENTS

I

THE FOUR NOBLE TRUTHS

THE FIRST TEACHING OF THE BUDDHA, soon after he attained awakening at Bodhgaya, was called the "Four Noble Truths." The Four Noble Truths are the fundamental teachings of Buddhism; they were realized, experienced, and taught by the Buddha himself. The Four Noble Truths encapsulate the true nature of life and the universe. They are:

1. Suffering
2. The cause of suffering
3. The cessation of suffering

4. The path leading to the cessation of suffering

The Four Noble Truths are the foundation of Buddhism, from which all other teachings are derived. The Four Noble Truths are often associated exclusively with Theravada Buddhism, but they are central to Mahayana Buddhism as well. The *Flower Adornment Sutra*, one of the most important sutras of Mahayana Buddhism, has a whole chapter dedicated to the Four Noble Truths. Thus, all Buddhists should learn the Four Noble Truths, for they are fundamental to Buddhism.

These four statements are called "truths" because we can investigate our world and see that they are true. The first noble truth is "suffering," which means seeing that this world is like a burning house, full of suffering and lacking in joy. The second noble truth is the "cause of suffering," which is realizing that the afflictions of greed, anger, and ignorance are the causes of birth, death, and suffering. The third noble truth is the "cessation of suffering," which is realized by attaining *nirvana*. The fourth noble truth is the "path leading to the cessation of suffering," which is the method to transcend the world of suffering and find real happiness, also known as the Noble Eightfold Path.

The first and second noble truths describe the formation of this mundane world of delusion: the second noble truth is the cause, while the first noble truth is the effect. In the same way, the third and fourth noble truths describe how we can enter the world of awakening: the fourth noble truth, the Noble Eightfold Path—when practiced, acts as the cause for the third noble truth—attaining *nirvana*. Let us look at the Four Noble Truths one by one.

1. The Truth of Suffering

We should have a joyful, optimistic, and positive outlook on life. We should not constantly talk about suffering, walk around with knitted eyebrows and sad expressions, or be consumed by depression and misery. However, after hearing the Four Noble Truths, some people may wonder: if we should seek happiness in life, then why does Buddhism dwell so much on suffering?

The Buddha talked about suffering because it is important for us to realize that all kinds of suffering really do exist in this world. Once we know the true nature of suffering, we can find a way to end it. Knowing that suffering exists is just the first step. The next step, learning how to be free from suffering, is the reason the Buddha talked about suffering.

Some people may think, "I do not want wealth or fame, nor am I hampered by love and emotion. I'm happy. Why does Buddhism say that life is full of suffering?"

There are many forms of suffering, some physical and some mental. Some people have less desire for material comforts and are able to withstand the hardships of extreme weather and accept the pain of poverty. Some can rise above the attachment of emotions, handle the agony of being separated from loved ones, and tolerate the hassle of dealing with people they do not like. But no one is free from the pain that occurs at the end of life. Therefore, everyone will experience some kind of suffering during his or her life. If we can fully understand the sources of suffering and overcome them, then we can free ourselves from the deep sea of suffering, and enjoy real happiness.

What, then, are the causes of suffering?

Material Things

The first cause of suffering is the disharmony between us and material things. For example, if we live in a small house with many people, we may feel cramped and this will cause us to suffer. If a pillow is too thick or too thin and we cannot sleep we will become restless, and then short-tempered. To a student, even the height of a desk or the brightness of a light can be a distraction and a source of discomfort.

Dissatisfaction with the material things in our everyday life can give rise to suffering. Not only things outside of ourselves, but even our skin, hair, and nails, if not taken care of properly, can become filthy and a source of distress. There is a Chinese proverb that says, "Our hair is like three thousand strands of trouble." Our lives are inextricably connected to material things.

People

The disharmony between people can be the greatest cause of affliction. We cannot always be with the people we love, yet we often have to deal with people we dislike.

Because of different views and attitudes, conflicts arise and suffering ensues. Sometimes, even when we are careful and try not to offend others, we still feel insecure when we see people whispering in a group, because we assume that they are criticizing us behind our backs. Disharmony in our relationships with other people can diminish our aspirations and result in a sense of dejection and apathy. That is why it is essential to establish harmonious relationships when we deal with others.

The Body

Some people say, "Health is wealth." This is true, for even if we possess all the treasures in the world and have unparalleled talents, we cannot accomplish anything without a healthy body. The aging, sickness, and death of the body is a natural cycle that no one can escape. A healthy person will become weak one day. A beautiful complexion will wither with age. We may flaunt our strength in our youth, but our bodies will inevitably deteriorate with time: our eyesight will worsen and our movements will slow down; even a minor cold can confine us to bed for several days; a minor toothache can make us toss and turn in our sleep.

The Mind

The mind likes to take control and be like a king, ruling over all its subjects. It is also like an untamed horse running wild, unwilling to be controlled. We try to take control of the mind but greed, anger, and ignorance resurface time and time again. Our efforts seem so futile. The suffering that comes from the mind can even exceed the suffering of the body. When the body becomes ill, we can cure it with medicine, but when the mind is sick, even the best physician may not know what to do.

People will often complain and say, "You're not listening to me!" But do you know who almost never listens? Your own mind. We often cannot stop the mind from wandering or creating mental afflictions. In this sense, our own mind can be our most formidable enemy. If we are constantly at odds with our own mind, suffering is inevitable.

Desire

As human beings, it is impossible for us to be completely without desire, but desires can be wholesome or unwholesome. Wholesome desires are those such as wanting to

14

become a sage or a Buddha, to excel in one's career, to serve one's community, or to benefit one's country and fellow human beings. On the other hand, coveting material comforts, grasping for power and position, or craving the pleasure of a love affair are unwholesome desires, and can lead to our downfall. Even wholesome desires, when managed improperly, can become overwhelming burdens and give rise to great suffering. Unwholesome desires are even more damaging! Thus, an important ingredient of success is to know how to transcend one's material desires.

Views

"View" refers to our way of thinking and our perceptions. While a lack of material things is tolerable, isolation due to one's views and solitude of the spirit are more difficult to bear. Since ancient times, many seekers of truth have found themselves alone on their journey. In fact, the Buddha almost decided not to teach, due to concern that living beings may not be able to understand the truth he had realized.

What leads us to suffer most are those views and concepts that seem correct but are actually wrong. During the Buddha's time, there were

ascetics who practiced self-morti-
fication. Some stood upside down
in the forest; some sat dangerous-
ly close to fires; some submerged
themselves in water; some refused
to eat; and some went about naked.

They believed that through
these methods they might be liberated from their bodies. Because of
their wrong views these ascetics in-
flicted physical pain on themselves
unnecessarily. Wrong views and
understanding can cause us much
suffering; they are the main stum-
bling blocks to our realization of
the truth.

Nature

In human history, our first struggles were between ourselves and the natural world. Since ancient times, the amount of suffering visited upon us by natural disasters such as hurricanes, earthquakes, and fires has been incalculable. When there is too much rain, the lowlands are flooded. When there is too little rain, drought cracks the soil and ruins the harvest.

The Self

The real root of suffering, whether caused by external factors such as material things and nature, or by internal factors such as the mind and our views, can be traced to our attachment to "I" and "mine." According to Buddhism, the source of all suffering is the illusory self, the "I." This "I" is but a combination of what the Buddha called the "five aggregates": form, feeling, perception, mental formations, and consciousness. When the five aggregates come together, they result in life, but they can only exist together as long as the proper conditions are present.

Nothing can exist unless the conditions for its existence are appropriate. Most of the time we act as though we will live forever. We cling to the body as the real self, generate all manner of craving, and create endless suffering. If we can see that this "self" is an illusion, then we can transcend all suffering. How can we do this? By realizing that all things, the five aggregates included, are empty of an independent "self." Let me illustrate what this means with the following example.

Soccer is a very popular sport around the world, and spectators at soccer matches often number in the tens of thousands. Among the spectators at one of these matches was a man who was smoking while watching the game. He was so absorbed in the game that he did not realize his cigarette was too close to the man next to him and it burned a hole in his neighbor's clothing.

"Ouch, that hurts!" the neighbor yelled.

The smoker then realized what he had done, and quickly apologized. The person whose clothing was burned was so caught up in the excitement of the game he said, "It doesn't matter. I'll buy another one later."

How would you describe the neighbor's state of mind? He was so focused on the match that he was in the state of "non-self," wherein watching the match was all that mattered to him. If he were not so caught up in the game, such an incident would have developed into a big fight. But, when both parties focused all their attention on watching which side was winning or losing, the concept of "self" no longer mattered.

Imagine: something as simple as a soccer match is enough to capture our attention, so much so that we can forget the "self" and pay little heed to a burning pain. If we can realize the emptiness of the five aggregates, we can definitely overcome all suffering.

The existence of suffering is an undeniable truth. We must understand suffering, and then take the next step to overcome this problem. Economics, medicine, and politics all seek to improve our life and minimize suffering. But unlike Buddhism, ordinary social welfare endeavors like aiding the poor and needy through charity can only give momentary relief. They do not remove suffering at its root cause.

Buddhism is about removing our present suffering, but more importantly, it teaches us how to eradicate the roots of suffering and liberate ourselves from the endless cycle of birth and death. Buddhism does not pessimistically accept suffering, but instead views it as a problem we must actively overcome.

Of course, believing in Buddhism does not prevent birth, aging, sickness, and death. But, when faced with such suffering, Buddhism can help grant us greater strength to overcome it, and when we come face to face with death, we will be able to accept it more openly and gracefully.

Many of the great awakened Buddhist masters chose to live in the forest, by the water, or even in cemeteries, in order to realize their Buddha nature. Many of the noble followers of Confucianism chose to leave the hustle and bustle of city life to lead a simple, honest, and tranquil life, without any worldly desires. Most people find such a lifestyle difficult to accept, but these sages willingly lived lives of simplicity, and in great happiness. Why? This was because they had such high aspirations for themselves. They had great confidence in their ideals, so they had the strength to endure the hardships and suffering that ordinary people cannot.

A proper understanding of religion will give us the strength to willingly overcome hardships. Many people pray to all varieties of gods asking for protection, money, wealth, health, and other things that they want. This kind of religion only encourages greed. When people don't get what they want, they despair, and may even blame the gods for their suffering. This kind of religion does not give people strength.

As Buddhists, we should not make unreasonable demands from the Buddhas and bodhisattvas. Instead we should follow the example of the Buddhas and bodhisattvas and dedicate ourselves to the benefit of all beings. This way we can have the strength to overcome our own afflictions and outside difficulties. If we can accept with equanimity when others are either nice or hostile to us, and if we can look at all worldly matters, be they bad or good, in the same way, then we can confront suffering with ease and calmness.

Though in Buddhism we talk about the suffering in life, I personally feel that life is full of joy. Why? When we can overcome suffering, then we can truly know joy. The fruit which ripens after diligent cultivation tastes especially sweet.

Cultivating strong faith can help us to transcend suffering.

Strong faith can help us to transcend the pain of suffering, but bringing an end to the more fundamental suffering that comes with birth and death is the ultimate goal of Buddhist practice. We should not be complacent just because we can deal with suffering through our willpower, mental adjustment, and thinking. Even if we have control over the minor afflictions of life, if we are not completely free from birth, aging, sickness, and death, then suffering still exists. A Chinese proverb says, "To catch a gang of thieves, one should catch their leader first." We must eradicate the root of suffering in order to attain lasting joy.

The root of suffering is "self"—attachment to the self, love for the self, and our self-centered views. Because of "self," we seek nice things to satisfy our needs, and this pursuit gives way to greed. When our greed cannot be satisfied, anger arises. When we cling to our deluded views without understanding the truth of the facts, ignorance arises. Because of "self," the fetters of greed, anger, and ignorance follow us like shadows.

How can we eradicate the root of suffering? If we can understand the truth of "non-self," then the root of suffering can be eradicated.

However, "non-self" does not mean that we have to destroy our lives; Buddhism is not nihilistic! Buddhism does not deny that life has value and meaning. "Non-self" means to free oneself from attachment to the self, the love of self, and the desires of the self. It does not mean we should destroy everything, or give up everything. Even if we were to commit suicide, death would only occur to this illusory body, not to our persistent clinging to the "self."

It is by letting go of our attachment to the "self" and wrong views that we can realize the truth. By letting go of our individual self with its greed, anger, and desires, we can come to know our true, pure, and joyous nature.

The noble men and women who realize their true selves do not leave the community. They still drink tea, eat meals, deal with other people, and handle matters; they still live normal lives. The only difference is that they have a pure state of mind. They have given up all kinds of obsessions and have realized the real nature of things. They are free from the suffering.

The "self" that we cling to so dearly is like a dream. Our life lasts only for a few decades; it is illusory, and changes constantly. The real "self" transcends time, space, and relativity. It is pure, and free from afflictions. To be free from suffering and attain joy we must expand our individual "self" and realize the boundless life of the true self.

2. The Truth of the Cause of Suffering

In Buddhism, "karma" refers to all that we do, say, and think. Throughout our lives, we create a lot of unwholesome karma because of our ignorant urges and cravings. Unwholesome karma is like a seed that bears the fruit of suffering. Thus, our suffering is caused by our own karma, as we are subject to the effects of whatever actions we have done. Karma does not disappear; it only accumulates. However, karma is not all bad. There is also wholesome karma. Whether we taste the fruit of suffering or of joy depends on the karmic seeds we sow.

Karma is a concept found in Buddhism as well as other Indian philosophies. However, the Buddha taught that we have the power to shape our karma and create a bright future for ourselves. Karma can be a source of hope. There are some who will ask, "Didn't you just say that karma is the cause of suffering? Now, why do you say it gives us hope? Isn't this contradictory?" If you truly understand the teaching of karma and how it works, you will not doubt that it is indeed very hopeful.

The essential teaching of karma is that everyone is responsible for his or her own actions. Throughout history, there has always been one inexplicable question that has confounded philosophers and religious thinkers alike: What is the origin of life and the universe? The Christian religion maintains that the world was created by God, while Brahmanism in India holds the view that everything evolved from Brahma. These religions, and others, attempt to explain the initial creation of life and the universe, and to establish a set of laws in which everything is controlled by a god.

Alternatively, Buddhism teaches us that human beings themselves, not someone else, are in charge of their own destinies. Even God or Brahma cannot escape their own karma. In Buddhism, the happiness or suffering in one's life, and the brightness or darkness of one's future is not bestowed by any god, but is instead determined by the efforts that we have made. Wholesome fruit is produced from the seeds of our wholesome deeds. Likewise, unwholesome fruit is produced from the seeds of our unwholesome deeds. No one can give us fortune or misfortune. We create our own good and bad actions; no one else controls us. Buddhism believes in free will. It is a religion that believes in self-discipline, and that one will reap the results of one's own actions.

Dr. Hu Shi, the great modern Chinese scholar, said, "Whatever harvest one wants, one must first plant accordingly." When we create karma it is like planting a seed. We have to sow the kind of seed that will produce the type of fruit we would like to harvest. No one is exempt from the effects of karma, even the rich and powerful. The effects of karma apply equally to everyone, regardless of position, gender, status, or wealth. Everyone will receive what they deserve and render their own karmic outcome. No one can take someone else's place, whether one is husband or wife, father or son, teacher or student, or one of our friends. Our karma is a clear record of our actions, so accurate that not even today's supercomputers can be compared to it.

If we do an unwholesome deed, an unwholesome karmic effect will follow. When this unwholesome karma comes to fruition it can cause us suffering, but there is still room for hope and a bright future.

It is similar to a person who borrows money from many people and is heavily in debt. After he repays all his debts, he will be free.

According to the Buddha's teachings, all phenomena are impermanent. Our unwholesome karma is not different: it is impermanent, empty, and without an independent "self." If we stop creating unwholesome karma and instead create wholesome karma, we will be free from suffering one day and can be truly happy.

Karma is neither pessimistic nor fatalistic; rather, it is optimistic and progressive. If we wish to be free from suffering, we must remove the causes of suffering and cease to generate unwholesome karma. Once we understand the causes of suffering, a joyful life will then no longer be out of reach.

3. THE TRUTH OF THE CESSATION OF SUFFERING

If someone were to ask, "Why become a Buddhist? What is the purpose of Buddhism?" How would you answer? If you ask me, my answer may frighten you, because I am a Buddhist for the sake of seeking "cessation."

The word "cessation" may lead people to think at first of annihilation, extermination, or nothingness, and make people fearful. In the history of Buddhism, there have been many cases in which the meaning of the Buddha's teaching was misinterpreted due to incorrect translations, and these mistakes became obstacles for Buddhism.

When a person hears the word "cessation," rather than thinking of annihilation or extermination, he or she should consider the real meaning of the word as used in the third noble truth, which is to rid oneself of the affliction of delusion and discrimination so that one's true nature is revealed just as it is. Thus, cessation in this case is not pessimistic nor destructive, but positive, creative, and constructive.

"Cessation" is the ideal state in which greed, anger, and ignorance have been completely eradicated. The quiet, peaceful state of *nirvana* will appear only when the fire of sensual desire is extinguished. Cessation means the extinction of birth and death and the severing of the cycle of birth and death. The cycle of birth and death is the reason for our suffering, which we must endure through long periods of anguish. By removing ourselves from this cycle we can attain freedom from birth and death. To do this, we must solve the problem at its root and extinguish our mundane desires.

When you hear that Buddhism advocates eliminating all desire, you may fear that this means a Buddhist can no longer marry, have children, make money, have a high position, or enjoy worldly pleasures. However, there is no need to worry. Buddhism is a religion that seeks peace and joy. It does not renounce normal living; what it rejects is overindulgence. In fact, as a Buddhist, one can still marry, do business, and live a normal life. There is a Buddhist sutra, the *Vimalakirti Sutra*, which describes a layman named Vimalakirti who was married and very well-to-do, yet was not a slave to material desire. In the sutra, he is described thus: "Though a layman, he is not attached to the three realms. Though married, he always cultivates purity."

There are those who say that Buddhism rejects affection. In reality, Buddhism strongly emphasizes affection; what Buddhism seeks to eliminate is selfish affection and desire. One should transform selfish affection into compassion and selfish desire into wisdom.

The affection advocated by Buddhism is devotion, not possession. It promotes the compassion of giving, not wanting. The love advocated by Buddhism is the love for all sentient beings, not just for one specific being. A bodhisattva's compassionate act of aiding all sentient beings is the manifestation of this selfless affection in its highest form. Affection that embodies compassion and wisdom will not go awry.

Some people seek out romantic love all their lives. Love can bring happiness, but it can also bring suf-

fering. When we read the news-
paper, we see that murders occur
every day. When we examine the
underlying causes of these crimes,
we see that relationships and money are usually the main causes. Love
without wisdom and compassion is
a very dangerous trap.

Some people think that happiness is nothing more than having
love and money. Buddhism, on the
other hand, says that people should
eliminate selfish affection and the
greed for money. What then is happiness in Buddhism?

Buddhism does not say that
money itself is the problem. Money

is not something dangerous. Being poor is not a sin, nor is being rich loathsome. In fact, according to the Mahayana bodhisattva path, as long as wealth does not give rise to greed, and as long as one's status can benefit Buddhism, wealth or a high position can be beneficial. Such things are neither innately good nor bad. The key lies in the way wealth and position are created and used.

Some people have the misconception that Buddhism says that we must renounce all possessions. This is simply not true. Actually, Buddhism says that it is important to have things; it is just that the things we should have are different from what people generally think they should have. According to Buddhism, what we should "have" is joy, not just for ourselves, but for all sentient beings. The way to accomplish this goal is to develop the mind of non-attachment—that is, to have everything by not possessing anything.

I often say that we should consider "not having" as "having," for we can only "have" things by "not having." When we possess things, they are by their nature limited, measurable, and calculable; whereas, "not having" is limitless, immeasurable, and boundless.

Within life there are two worlds. The one before our eyes is a narrow "world of possessing." Because of ignorance, sentient beings fight for these possessions. They do not know that when they turn around, they will find that there is another, larger world behind them. This is the "world of not having," which can only be realized when we remove our selfishness and desires. In this world of "not having," there is no birth and death, desires are extinguished, and all duality, differences, and illusions no longer exist. It is a completely liberated and carefree state of being. This is the state that all Buddhists should strive to attain.

When do we attain this liberated state? Must we wait until after death? No. This very state was attained by the Buddha as he sat beneath the bodhi tree on the night of his awakening. If we work diligently, we can attain this state, just as the Buddha did.

What is the state of an awakened being? To most people, an awakened person may seem very strange. In the Chan School of Buddhism, the school which emphasizes meditation and direct mind-to-mind transmission of the teachings, awakened masters are said to have expressed themselves in many different ways upon attaining awakening. Some laughed madly, and others even struck their masters. The masters did not mind such behavior; in fact, they actually approved of it. While unacceptable for an ordinary person, this kind of behavior from an awakened being denotes the nature of Chan.

4. The Truth of the Path Leading to the Cessation of Suffering

The Buddha described the method for removing the causes of suffering in great detail. Some of these teachings include the four immeasurable states of mind, the four universal vows, the threefold training, the five precepts, the ten wholesome actions, the seven limbs of enlightenment, the Noble Eightfold Path, the thirty-seven practices to enlightenment, and the six perfections. All of these are considered part of the method to remove the causes of suffering. But, for the sake of brevity, it is best to focus on the Noble Eightfold Path.

The Noble Eightfold Path includes eight factors that, when practiced correctly, lead to the cessation of suffering. These steps are: right view, right thought, right speech, right action, right livelihood, right effort, right mindfulness, and right meditative concentration. The Noble Eightfold Path appears to be very simple, but to understand it thoroughly can be difficult. Let us take a look at each of the elements in the Noble Eightfold Path.

Right View

Right view is what enables us to maintain our faith in the truth when faced with inequalities or difficulties. Worldly knowledge can be both good and bad. Sometimes it is not reliable and can mislead us. Consider for a moment the Chinese character for ignorance *chi*:

This character is a compound of two other characters: *zhi* (知), which means knowledge, and *chuang* (疒), which means ailment.

When knowledge is corrupted, it turns into ignorance. Some people are extremely clever, but when they do bad things, it is doubly destructive! For example, both Nazi Germany's Hitler and the first emperor of the Qin dynasty were clever yet diabolical. A person's knowledge is not necessarily proportional to his morality. Knowledge is like a sharp knife; if not used properly it can hurt others. That is why we must transform knowledge into wisdom and right view.

Transforming knowledge into wisdom and right view is not easy. The principle is the same as in taking photographs. The focus, distance, and shutter speed must be adjusted accordingly before one can take a clear and beautiful picture. Similarly, one can see the true nature of life and the universe as it really is only if one has the right view. If one lacks the right view when observing this earthly world, serious mistakes will be made. It is like peering at flowers through a heavy fog, or like a group of blind people touching different parts of an elephant and trying to convince each other what the animal is like.

Right Thought

Right thought is right volition, decision, and contemplation. It means not having thoughts of greed, anger, and ignorance, which are the main obstacles to awakening. These three poisons continually occupy our minds and contaminate our pure nature. It is not easy to be rid of greed, anger, and ignorance. We have to exert constant effort to maintain the right thinking necessary to attain Buddhahood.

Right Speech

Using right speech means that we should not lie, slander others, use harsh language, or utter frivolous speech. There is a Chinese proverb that says, "Illness comes from what you eat. Trouble comes from what you say." Our own speech can not only hurt others, it can hurt ourselves too. Thus, it is very important that we choose our words wisely.

Right Action

Right action means that we should not kill, steal, engage in sexual misconduct, or consume intoxicants of any kind. Besides abstaining from doing unwholesome deeds, we also need to actively perform wholesome deeds.

Right Livelihood

Right livelihood refers to the proper way of making a living. This is accomplished by abstaining from unethical jobs such as operating gambling houses, selling alcoholic beverages and weapons, and operating slaughterhouses. Also, part of right livelihood is having well-disciplined habits, such as getting an adequate amount of sleep, food, exercise, rest, and work. Right livelihood not only promotes efficiency and health, it also enables us to have a stable society and a joyous family life.

Right Effort

Right effort means to apply our effort in four areas: 1) to not produce unwholesome qualities that have not been produced; 2) to eliminate the unwholesome qualities that already exist; 3) to nurture wholesome qualities that have not yet been produced; and 4) to maintain and multiply the wholesome qualities that already exist.

Right Mindfulness

To have right mindfulness is to keep one's attention, awareness, and mind focused on the four foundations of mindfulness: 1) the body is impure; 2) feelings will always result in suffering; 3) the mind is impermanent; 4) all phenomena do not have a substantial self. If we always contemplate the meaning of impermanence, suffering, and non-self, we will not be greedy for the trifles of this world; we will instead strive diligently for the truth.

Right Meditative Concentration
Right concentration refers to the four stages of meditative concentration (*dhyana*). In short, to develop right meditative concentration means to focus our will and our thoughts through meditation.

The Four Noble Truths are similar to the process a doctor goes through when treating a patient. The first noble truth, suffering, is the patient's symptoms. The second noble truth, the cause of suffering, is the doctor's diagnosis. The fourth noble truth, the Noble Eightfold Path, is the treatment the doctor recommends. The third noble truth, cessation, is when the patient is cured. The ailments of the body are cured by medicine, but the ailments of the mind are cured with Buddhism.

After his awakening, the Buddha taught the Four Noble Truths he had discovered. The first time he taught the Dharma, he "turned the wheel of Dharma" three times, emphasizing three different aspects of the Four Noble Truths. The first turning was instructive; he taught about the definitions and content of the Four Noble Truths. He explained, "Such is suffering, which is oppressive; such is the cause of suffering, which beckons; such is the cessation of suffering, which is attainable; such is the path, which can be practiced."

The second turning of the wheel was to provide encouragement. The Buddha persuaded his students to practice the Four Noble Truths to eradicate afflictions and attain awakening. He told them, "Such is suffering, you should understand it; such is the cause of suffering, you should end it; such is the cessation of suffering, you should realize it; such is the path, you should practice it."

In the third turning, the Buddha told his students that he himself had realized the Four Noble Truths. He encouraged all sentient beings to put forth their best effort and strive to realize the Four Noble Truths, just as he had done himself. The Buddha said, "Such is suffering,

I have understood it; such is the cause of suffering, I have ended it; such is the cessation of suffering, I have realized it; such is the path, I have practiced it."

II

THE DOCTRINES OF BUDDHISM

EVERY RELIGION OR PHILOSOPHY has its own set of doctrines, and Buddhism does as well. Many Buddhist doctrines are quite different from other religions and unique to Buddhism. Some of these characteristic doctrines are listed below.

KARMA

Karma, as previously mentioned, is one of the most fundamental teachings of Buddhism. Among all Buddhist doctrines, it is the most important while, at the same time, often the most misunderstood.

Karma is a Sanskrit word that means "action" or "deed." Any intentional physical, verbal, or mental action is karma. As an umbrella term, karma can also be used to refer to not only one's intentional actions, but the responses and effects of these actions.

Karma can be generated by one's body, speech, and mind. Some examples of unwholesome karma created by the body are killing, stealing, and sexual misconduct. Unwholesome karma created by speech includes lying, flattery, duplicity, and harsh speech. Unwholesome karma created by the mind includes greed, hatred, and ignorance. However, "karma" refers to more than just unwholesome karma. The karma of body, speech, and mind creates happiness in our lives as well as sorrow. Let us talk about the different types of karma.

Broadly speaking there is wholesome karma, unwholesome karma, and neutral karma, which is neither wholesome nor unwholesome. Wholesome karma are those actions which are moral and benefit others. Unwholesome karma are those actions which harm others. Any action which does not have a moral component, which cannot be said to be good or bad, is neutral karma.

When we perform wholesome or unwholesome actions, they are stored as karmic seeds within our *alaya* consciousness, which acts as a storehouse for all of our karma. When the right conditions are present, these karmic seeds will generate karmic effects. Wholesome karmic effects provide us with blessings in our lives and lead to rebirth in the higher realms. Unwholesome karmic effects bring suffering in our lives and lead to rebirth in the lower realms. Those beings who have attained great degrees of meditative concentration may also be reborn in the form or formless realms, where beings are constantly absorbed in states of meditative bliss.

Karma can also be divided according to the time that it's effects reach fruition. Karmic effects can ripen in this life, in the next life, or in future lives beyond the next. Across the past, present, and future, karma is never lost or forgotten. Karmic effects mature at different rates, just like some crops are ready to harvest in a single season, while others require several seasons before they are ready.

Those who do not understand karma may see kind people who suffer misfortune and wicked people who live comfortably and think that karma must not exist. Such people may say, "We are living in the twenty-first century. Why still believe in old-fashioned superstitions like the law of karma?" However, the relationship between karmic causes and effects are very complicated. In fact, all of existence arises in dependence on karma, and does so in a very orderly and precise manner.

Karmic effects ripen at different times for two main reasons. The first reason is how weighty the karmic cause is. The second is the strength of the conditions necessary to bring about the effect. That being said, all wholesome and unwholesome karma will eventually produce karmic effects. It is just a matter of time.

A good person who is suffering in this life suffers because the karma from previous lives is finally producing effects now. Even though he does wholesome deeds in this life, they may not ripen and produce karmic effects until the next life. The bad person who lives an easy life is enjoying the wholesome karma of previous lives that is only now producing effects, but the unwholesome karma that he is creating in his present life will still ripen and mature one day.

Karma is inevitable. Once something is done, wholesome or unwholesome, the seeds of karma are stored in the *alaya* consciousness and will one day produce effects when the conditions are right. Wholesome and unwholesome karma also do not "cancel each other out." Unwholesome karma will produce unwholesome effects. These effects cannot be removed by doing good deeds. The only thing that can be done is to do more good deeds to generate positive conditions. The severity of the effects of unwholesome karma can be lessened, or wholesome effects can be caused to ripen more quickly.

Consider the following: A glass of water has some salt added to it until the water tastes salty. The salt is similar to unwholesome karma. If we add fresh water, similar to wholesome karma, the salt water becomes diluted so that it tastes less salty. That is why it is important to do wholesome deeds and create positive conditions.

Some people may say, "I have been a vegetarian my whole life, but what do I have to show for it? I've gone bankrupt!" or "I have been bowing to the Buddha and reciting Amitabha Buddha's name for a long time, yet my health has not improved!"

Such people do not understand karma. Morality is governed by its own causes and effect, finances are governed by their own causes and effects, and health is governed by its own separate causes and effects. If you want to be healthy, you need to pay attention to what you eat, get an adequate amount of exercise and maintain good hygiene. If you do not pay attention to these things and simply believe that reciting Amitabha Buddha's name will give you good health, you do not understand karma.

If you want to be financially successful, then you must practice sound business management. You cannot expect to become wealthy just because you are a vegetarian. Again, this is a misunderstanding of karma. People need to understand that most things in life do not come free. Believing in the Buddha will not help you achieve your goals. Effort and results are directly proportional and one needs to put in a sufficient amount of effort for a certain amount of results. Even if a modern electronic calculator or computer were used to add up the wholesome and unwholesome deeds committed by a person, it would not be as accurate as the law of karma.

Karmic retributions that manifest at the time of death can be divided into weighty karma, habitual karma, and recollective karma. Weighty karma means that if a person has performed both wholesome and unwholesome karma, then whichever is heavier will manifest first.

Habitual karma will also manifest itself, according to one's daily habits. The Pure Land School of Buddhism teaches people to recite Amitabha Buddha's name, so that this practice will become a habit and that at the time of passing away, the Pure Land practitioner will recite Amitabha Buddha's name and thus be reborn in the Pure Land.

Recollective karma means that one's karma is manifested according to one's memory. For example, when a person is on the street and comes to a crossroad, he may be at a loss as to which direction he should go. Suddenly, he remembers that he has a friend on the street that leads west, so he continues in a westerly direction. Thus he may be guided by his recollective karma in a similar fashion.

Whether or not a person is reborn as a human is determined by his or her own karma. We are born as human beings as a result of our previous karma. In other words, karma is the strong force that drives us to be reborn in our present lives as human beings, instead of being reborn as dogs or horses. Though we are all human beings, we nonetheless have individual differences, such as being intelligent or foolish, virtuous or unruly, rich or poor, or being born into noble or humble circumstances. These variations are due to differences in the past karma performed by each of us during our past lives. Those who were generous in their previous lives will become rich, while those who have killed others will consequently have a short lifespan. The karma that "fills in the details" of our rebirths is called completing karma.

Karma can also be divided into the categories of collective and individual karma: the karma performed by a single person will give rise to a certain force; the karma performed by hundreds and thousands of people will give rise to a greater force;

the karma performed by millions and billions of people will give rise to an even greater force. These latter two forces are called collective karma.

The collective behavior of many beings will produce a very strong karmic effect that determines the course of life, history, and the universe. Individual karma differs from collective karma in that it only affects the individual. For example, people experience natural disasters such as famines and earthquakes if they live in the disaster area. The disasters are manifested due to the collective karma of the people within the disaster area. However, during the same disaster, each person may be affected differently, due to his or her own individual karma.

DEPENDENT ORIGINATION

"Dependent origination" is the Buddhist doctrine that all phenomena arise due to causes and conditions. During the Buddha's forty-nine year teaching career he gave special attention to the doctrine of dependent origination, for it is one of the features that distinguishes Buddhism from other religions.

Dependent origination states that, since all phenomena arise due to causes and conditions, all existence in the universe is interdependent. From something as large as the universe to something as small as a speck of dust or a blade of grass, all arise due to causes and conditions.

This principle cannot be understood through academic knowledge alone. It has to be experienced and realized through actual practice. Before the Buddha renounced secular life, he was already very well versed in the philosophy of the four Vedas, the classical Indian five sciences (composition, mathematics, medicine, logic, and philosophy), and the many practices and meditation techniques of the various mendicant religions. But he only realized the truth of dependent origination upon attaining Buddhahood.

During the time of the Buddha there was a brahman named Sariputra who had practiced Brahmanism for a long time and had many followers but who still had not realized the truth. One day, Sariputra was walking on a street in Rajagrha and met Asvajit, one of the Buddha's first five disciples. Asvajit was deeply influenced by

the Buddha's teachings and always
practiced what the Buddha taught.
Asvajit's demeanor and outward
appearance earned him the respect
of people who saw him. Sariputra
asked him respectfully, "Who are
you? Who is your teacher? What
does he teach you?"

Asvajit replied, "All phenomena
arise due to causes and conditions;
all phenomena cease due to causes
and conditions. Lord Buddha, the
great sage, always teaches thus."

Sariputra was overjoyed when
he heard this. He imparted the
wonderful news to his good friend,
Maudgalyayana. The two of them,

together with all of their respective followers, went to follow the Buddha. Among the disciples, Sariputra became the foremost in great wisdom, while Maudgalyayana became the most prominent in supernatural powers, all of which arose from that one teaching on dependent origination.

There are three primary principles of dependent origination:

1. Effects Arise from Causes

No phenomena can exist without suitable causes and conditions. In this instance, a "cause" is the direct force which brings about an effect, while a "condition" is a secondary, indirect factor which contributes to an effect.

No phenomena simply arises by itself. For example, let us consider a soybean. The soybean is a seed, the main cause. Water, soil, sunlight, air, and fertilizer are the necessary secondary conditions. If these causes and conditions come together in an appropriate manner, then the seed can germinate, bloom, and produce fruit. Thus the fruit arises from causes. If we store this soybean in a granary or place it on gravel, it will always remain a seed. The seed cannot grow and bear fruit in the absence of the necessary external conditions.

When we look at society over a long period of time, it may seem like the status of a society in any given period has nothing to do with society as it was or as it will later become. But with careful analysis, we can see that each societal moment cannot arise without the society of the previous moment.

Let us take the example of a torch. When the flame from one torch is passed on to a new torch, the previous and the subsequent torches are two separate entities. However, there is a very subtle relationship between these two torches. The flame of the new torch is a continuation of the flame of the old torch. In the flow of time, it is impossible to find an entity isolated from all other entities.

Sometimes two things may seem like they have no relationship at all, but if we look carefully we can see the causes and conditions that connect the two phenomena. For example, when I go and give a Dharma talk, it is only able to happen because of many different causes and conditions. Someone needs to invite me, I must be available, the venue must be open, and the audience must be interested enough to come. Only when these all come together can the talk happen. If even a single one was lacking, it would not be possible.

When we talk about the formation of life, which came first–the chicken or the egg? If the chicken came first and the egg came later, then where did the chicken come from? If the egg came first and the chicken came later, then where did the egg come from?

For example, the clock on the wall runs continuously from one o'clock to twelve o'clock and from twelve o'clock back to one o'clock.

Which is the beginning? Which is the end? It is very difficult to say, because there is no beginning and no end. From this we can understand that causes and conditions are interdependent and interrelated. The best summary of depended origination, offered by the Buddha himself, is "This is, therefore that is; this arises, therefore that arises; this is not, therefore that is not; this ceases, therefore that ceases."

2. All Phenomena Arise According to Principles

Dependent Origination is subtle and profound, and can be difficult to understand. It cannot be analyzed using scientific techniques, nor can it be clarified by the metaphysics of philosophy. It is a truth of the universe that cannot be found in secular teachings. In the *Agamas*, the Buddha said that dependent origination is a unique characteristic of Buddhism.

Dependent origination states that all phenomena arise according to principles, the most fundamental principle being the law of karma. For example, the Buddha said that all that arises will one day cease. From the viewpoint of time, this statement can apply in the past, present, and future. From the viewpoint of space, this statement is true in every part of the world. Regardless of how developed we are culturally or how advanced we are technologically, we cannot escape the fact that anything which arises will eventually cease. Nothing that is contrary to this principle can exist. This is what is meant when we say, "All phenomena arise according to principles."

Another principle is that a given cause will generate a particular effect. This is the way it has always been, it will inevitably occur in this way, and it is so universally. Truth cannot be modified via debates and need not be described in words. It simply is.

3. Existence Arises from Emptiness

Where did this all come from? According to dependent origination, all phenomena arise from emptiness. Without emptiness, all phenomena would not exist. Why? Because without emptiness, there can be no existence. In its Buddhist usage, "emptiness" does not mean nothingness, but the "empty nature" of all phenomena. Without their empty nature, phenomena would be unable to manifest their functions.

Some people misunderstand emptiness as meaning that Buddhists must give up everything. However, according to Buddhism, "emptiness" is the basis of all existence. For example, there is a lot of empty space in the human body. We are only alive because there is some empty space in our ears and some empty space in our digestive system. If the nose, mouth, and stomach were not empty, how could we survive?

If a bed is not empty, then it cannot hold anything. If the universe is not empty, then human life cannot exist. Thus, there is existence only if there is emptiness. Without emptiness, all phenomena could not arise from conditions, and thus there would be no arising or ceasing of anything.

Based on this phenomenon of existence, in the chapter on the Four Noble Truths in the *Treatise on the Middle Way*, Nagarjuna said, "Because there is emptiness, all phenomena can arise; if there is no emptiness, all phenomena cannot arise."

EMPTINESS

Ordinary people often misunderstand emptiness and think it is the same as nothingness. This is a misconception. We have already mentioned the phenomenon of dependent origination, in which all phenomena arise and cease due to causes and conditions. When the proper causes and conditions come together, phenomena arise, and when these same causes and conditions come apart, phenomena cease. Because these phenomena are merely an assembly of other factors, they lack an intrinsic nature, and are thus "empty."

Most people think that existence is firm, solid, and real. According to Buddhism, it is temporary and illusory, as it comes into existence because of dependent origination. But existence does not preclude emptiness. In the same way the presence of emptiness as the nature of all things does not preclude existence. Dependent origination and emptiness affirm one another.

I would like to describe how emptiness interrelates with other Buddhist concepts and provides descriptions and examples of how the concept of emptiness is viewed in daily life:

1. The Four Great Elements and the Five Aggregates

In Mahayana Buddhism, emptiness has the meaning of infinity, not of nothingness. Emptiness is constructive, and accounts for the existence of the world and the universe. The Buddha said that the four great elements and the five aggregates, the constituent components of reality, are all empty.

All phenomena are formations of the four great elements. What are they? They are earth, water, fire and wind. Earth has the property of solidity, water has the property of fluidity, fire has the property of heat, and wind has the property of mobility.

Consider how a cup is made. A cup is produced by firing clay that is molded into the shape of a cup. The main ingredient, clay, belongs to the earth element. Water is then added to the clay in order to make the clay malleable. The cup is then fired in order to solidify its shape. Finally, the cup is cooled and dried by the wind. Even something as simple as making a cup involves all four elements.

The human body is also formed by the unity of the four great elements. For example, our skin, hair, nails, teeth, bones, and flesh all belong to the earth element. Our blood, saliva, and urine belong to the water element. Our body heat belongs to the fire element and our breathing and movement belong to the wind element. Thus, if any one of these four great elements is out of balance, we will become ill. If these four great elements disintegrate, we will no longer exist.

As we can see, our bodies are a combination of the four great elements. The body and the mind together are made up of the five aggregates: form, feeling, perception, mental formations, and consciousness. Life is a combination of many causes and conditions without a true, independent intrinsic nature.

Su Dongpo was a notable Chinese scholar and poet during the Song dynasty who maintained a close friendship with the great Chan Master Foyin. Once, Su Dongpo went to visit the Chan master when he was teaching the Dharma. When the Chan master saw Su Dongpo, he said to him, "Mr. Su, where did you just come from? We do not have a place for you to sit."

Su Dongpo replied immediately, "Master, if there is no seat, why don't you lend me your four great elements and five aggregates to use as my meditation seat?"

Chan Master Foyin said, "I have a question for you. If you can give me a satisfactory answer, I will let you use me as your seat. If you cannot give me an answer, then please leave your jade belt behind as a souvenir. Here is my question: my four great elements are all empty and my five aggregates do not have true existence. May I ask where you are going to sit?"

Su Dongpo could not give him an answer. So he took off his jade belt, which had been bestowed to him by the emperor, and left.

2. Defining Emptiness

Most people do not understand emptiness. They think it means complete nullity and nothingness. This is not so. Emptiness is, in fact, a most profound and wonderful philosophy. If one can truly understand emptiness, one can understand the entirety of Buddhism. What, then, is emptiness? It is simply not possible to explain the meaning of emptiness in just one sentence. The

Explanation of the Treatise on the Awakening of Faith in Mahayana lists ten definitions of emptiness. Although these definitions cannot thoroughly explain the true meaning of emptiness, they are close approximations:

a) Emptiness obstructs nothing. It pervades everything but obstructs nothing.
b) Emptiness embraces all places. It spreads everywhere and there is nowhere it is not present.
c) Emptiness is equality. It has no preference for one thing over another.

d) Emptiness is immense. It is vast, without limits and boundaries.
e) Emptiness is formless, it has no shape or form.
f) Emptiness is pure, and is without defilement.
g) Emptiness is motionless. It is always still. It is not born and does not die, and does not arise nor cease.
h) Emptiness is unlimited. It completely negates all things that have limits.
i) Emptiness is empty. It completely negates the substantial existence of all things and destroys all attachments to it.

j) Emptiness cannot be clung to, caught, or held.

Although no single definition can entirely describe the truth of emptiness, together these ten definitions provide a vivid depiction for us to better understand how important the concept of emptiness is in Buddhist teaching.

3. *Perceiving Emptiness*

How can we come to know emptiness? We can actually recognize emptiness from observing existence. The following are seven such approaches:

Emptiness can be known from the continuous succession of events. All things are impermanent, and time marches on without interruption. As the march of impermanence continues, we can know emptiness.

Emptiness can be known by observing natural cycles. All things are governed by cause and effect: a seed is a cause which generates a fruit as an effect. The seeds in that fruit in turn become the causes for future effects. When we see that cause becomes effect and effect becomes cause, we can know emptiness.

Emptiness can be known from the compounding of various elements. All phenomena are made up of many component parts. For example, the human body is made from skin, flesh, bones, blood, and various fluids. If each of these parts was separated, no "human body" that existed apart from the components could be found.

Emptiness can be known through the relative nature of phenomena. All phenomena are defined by how they relate to one another, just as a father is a father because he has a son, and a teacher is a teacher because he has students. But when a son gets married and has children of his own, he too becomes a father. Likewise, a student who learns well can become a teacher. Thus, each of these is relative and empty.

Emptiness can be known through the lack of absolute standards. For example, if we see the light from a candle in the darkness we may say that the light is bright, but if we were to turn on an electric light the candle may then seem dim. We may say that the speed of an automobile is very fast, but it is slow when compared with the speed of an airplane. With no set standard, we can see each of these qualifications as being empty.

Emptiness can be known through the temporary nature of names. Each thing in the universe has a name, but these names are non-substantial, and thus are empty. For example, a female baby is called a baby girl. When she has grown up, she is referred to as "Miss." When she gets married, she will be addressed as "Mrs." When she has her own children, they will call her "mother." When she is old and has grandchildren, she is then known as a grandmother. From a baby girl to a grandmother, she is still the same person, though her name has changed.

Emptiness can be known through seeing the difference in perspectives. Different people with different states of mind will have unique views of the same thing or event. For example, on a snowy night, a poet sitting in front of the window inside a warm and cozy house hopes that the snow will continue through the night, so that he can enjoy more beautiful scenery. In contrast, a homeless person shivering in the cold hopes that the snow will soon stop; otherwise, he may not be able to make it through the night.

THE THREE DHARMA SEALS

The three Dharma seals are a Buddhist doctrine which is used to test the veracity of other doctrines. If a given teaching is marked by the three Dharma seals, it is a true teaching of the Buddha. If a teaching is not marked by the three Dharma seals, it is not a true teaching. The three Dharma seals are: All conditioned phenomena are impermanent, all phenomena are without an independent self, and *nirvana* is perfect tranquility.

1. All Conditioned Phenomena Are Impermanent

"All conditioned phenomena" is really another way of saying "everything in the world." According to Buddhism, nothing is permanent. All conditioned phenomena are impermanent in two ways: first, because they are in a constant state of flux as they flow from the past, to the present, to the future, and secondly because they arise due to causes and conditions and disperse due to causes and conditions.

The mind is also impermanent. Our thoughts change every moment, constantly arising and ceasing. All phenomena in the universe arise and cease from moment to moment. Their existence is a continuous process. Phenomena arise, abide, change, and cease. The seasons change from spring, summer, autumn, and winter. Life moves from birth, aging, sickness, to death. All of these continue on like a flowing river. Nothing ever remains unchanged in this continuous flux.

Buddhism says there are three types of feelings: pleasant feelings, painful feelings, and feelings that are neither pleasant nor painful. Painful feelings cause suffering, but pleasant feelings bring suffering as well, because they are subject to decay. For example, health and beauty will give rise to pleasant feelings, but the loss of health and beauty can cause suffering.

Even feelings that are neither pleasant nor painful can bring us suffering because of change. Examples of these kinds of feeling are those caused by the passing of time, the shortness of life, and the impermanence of all phenomena. All these perpetual changes bring people unbearable anguish—this is the suffering of impermanence. This is why the Buddhist teachings state that because all conditioned phenomena are impermanent, all feelings are suffering.

2. All Phenomena Are Without an Independent Self

Human beings like to cling to the "self." We believe that the "I" and "my" exist—*my* head, *my* body, *my* thoughts, *my* parents, *my* spouse and children. We see these things as ours, and cling to them. Consequently, we become overly protective of what we see as ours. We look at the world and locate the "I" as the center of the universe, as if nothing would exist without "I." However, according to the rational, penetrating perspective of the Buddhist teachings, there is actually no such thing as a permanent and independent "self." Why? For any entity to be called "self," it should fulfill four requirements: it must be permanent, in control, unchanging, and independent.

Let us now consider the human body, the entity that we tend to regard as "I." From the moment of birth, and continuing throughout the decades of a person's lifetime, the human body is perpetually undergoing the physiological changes of birth and death as it grows, matures, and ages. How, then, can it be permanent and unchanging? Formed from the four great elements and five aggregates, the human body comes into being when these conditions are present in their proper proportion, and ceases to be when that balance is no longer present.

How then can the human body be in control? The human body is where all varieties of suffering assemble—physical suffering such as hunger, cold, illness, fatigue, and mental suffering that includes anger, hatred, sorrow, fear, and disappointment. When the body is undergoing all these sufferings, it simply cannot break free. How can it be independent and have control? Therefore, we can see that the "self" as we have defined it earlier does not exist. Hence the Buddhist teachings state that all phenomena do not have an independent self.

The absence of an independent self is the foundation of the Middle Way; it is the fundamental teaching of Buddhism. The absence of an independent self is the unique teaching that differentiates Buddhism from other religious or philosophical doctrines.

3. Nirvana is Perfect Tranquility

This means that no matter how chaotic things are in this world, they will eventually become tranquil. No matter how different things are, they will eventually become equal in the end. Indeed, the state of *nirvana* is tranquil. According to Buddhism, when the state of *nirvana* is attained, all afflictions and the cycle of birth and death are extinguished; there will be no more suffering, equanimity will be attained, perfect wisdom will be realized, and all delusion will be eradicated.

Ordinary people think that *nirvana* is attained only after death.

Actually, *nirvana* is "without birth or death." *Nirvana* is the end of clinging, the elimination of the attachment to the "self" and the concept that things are real. It is the end of defilement and the hindrance of worldly knowledge. *Nirvana* is liberation. Defilement is bondage.

A criminal chained and in shackles has lost his freedom. Likewise, living beings are bound by the chains of greed, hatred, and ignorance. If living beings practice the Dharma and put an end to these defilements, then they will all be liberated and thus attain *nirvana*.

Nirvana is not to be gained in any other way.

During the Buddha's time, when one of the Buddha's disciples attained *nirvana* they would travel to different places to teach. From their example we can see that *nirvana* is not something attained apart from all other phenomena. All phenomena are originally *nirvana*.

However, because the mind is obscured by ignorance, delusion, clinging, and the supposition that the "self" and phenomena are real, we encounter obstacles, hindrances, and bondage everywhere they go.

If we can be like the Buddhist sages who understand that all things arise due to dependent origination, then even though we still exist in this world, we can realize that all existence is ever-changing and lacks true intrinsic nature. We will no longer be attached; wherever we are, we will be liberated. Liberation is *nirvana*.

Some people say that life is like an ocean in which there is perpetual motion, with waves coming one after the other. The continuous movement of the ocean exemplifies the impermanence of conditioned phenomena. If we can look at the waves through the eyes of the Buddhist sages, we then soon realize that although the waves are turbulent, the nature of water is always calm.

Likewise, life is an endless cycle of birth and death, but real intrinsic nature is always abiding in a state of perfect peace. Thus, if we want to attain the liberation of *nirvana*, we have to realize it through the impermanence and non-substantiality of conditioned phenomena. It is impossible to find the state of perfect equanimity of *nirvana* apart from impermanence and non-substantiality.

III

CAUSE AND CONDITION

THE BUDDHIST TEACHINGS differ from academic knowledge. Academic knowledge typically focuses on the explanation of appearances. It is an interpretation of reality based on name and form. In contrast, Buddhism teaches us to develop a penetrative understanding of the nature of phenomena that is perfect and complete.

Consider the human hand. Common knowledge simply says that it is a hand. Medical science looks at it as a structure of bones, muscles, nerves, and cells. Literature defines the hand in terms of style, gesture, and expression. A philosophical analysis of the hand sees it as a symbol of destiny and friendship. In physics, the opening and closing of the hand is describes by its forces and movement. In each analysis, the hand is regarded as real. The hand exists.

In contrast, the Buddhist view of the human hand penetrates its essence. This view sees the hand itself as an illusory and temporary form, unstable in nature, which will eventually decay and vanish. As a phenomenon, the hand is empty.

Suppose one were to extend the hand and make a grasping motion. Common knowledge would say the hand moved and that some air and dust were grasped. The *Diamond Sutra* says that such things are, "like dreams, illusions, bubbles, and shadows, like dew and lightning." The grasp only exists because of the combination of certain causes and conditions.

The human perspective is narrow and confined, and can hinder us from looking at the world with wisdom. Worldly happiness and suffering do not have an absolute existence of their own. They arise because of the discriminations we make through our perceptions and thinking. To understand and accept the Buddhist teachings, we need to change our perspectives. We must go beyond the superficial to see things as they really are, illuminate our wisdom, and sow the seeds of awakening. Only then will the water of the Dharma flow into the spiritual fields of our minds.

The following story makes this point: Once there was an old lady who cried all the time. Her elder daughter was married to an umbrella merchant while her younger daughter was the wife of a noodle vendor. On sunny days, she worried, "Oh no! The weather is so nice and sunny. No one is going to buy any umbrellas. What will happen if my eldest daughter's shop has to be closed?" Her worries upset her, and she could not help but cry.

When it rained, she would cry for the younger daughter. She thought, "Oh no! My younger daughter is married to a noodle vendor. You cannot dry noodles without the sun. Now there will be no noodles to sell. What will she do?" As a result, the old lady lived in sorrow every day. Whether sunny or rainy, she grieved for one of her daughters. Her neighbors could not console her and jokingly called her "the crying lady."

One day, she met a monk. He was very curious as to why she was always crying. She explained the problem to him. The monk smiled kindly and said, "Madam, do not worry. I will show you the way to happiness, and you will not need to grieve anymore."

The crying lady was very excited. She immediately asked the monk to show her what to do. The master replied, "It is very simple. You just need to change your perspective. On sunny days, do not think of your elder daughter not being able to sell umbrellas. Instead think of your younger daughter who will be able to dry her noodles. With such good strong sunlight, she will be able to make plenty of noodles and her business will be very good. When it rains, think about your elder daughter's umbrella store. With the rain, everyone must buy umbrellas. She will sell a lot of umbrellas and her store will prosper."

The old lady understood and followed the monk's instruction. After a while, she did not cry anymore; instead, she was smiling every day.

From that day on she was known as "the smiling lady."

When we have worries and problems, if we all emulate "the crying lady" and change our perspective a little, we can transform negativity into happiness and good fortune. This does not require magical power. If we can understand a little bit of the Dharma and apply it to our lives effectively, we will make breakthroughs in our understanding. Delusion will become wisdom, and ignorance will become enlightenment.

If we understand and live by the truths of cause and condition, and dependent origination, we can be just like the Buddha. We will be able to abandon all the pain and anxiety associated with this imperfect worldly existence. The sutras say, "All phenomena arise out of causes and conditions, and all phenomena cease due to causes and conditions."

But what is meant by "cause" and "condition"? We can learn about cause and condition by looking at human interactions and relationships. Relationships can be loving and respectful, antagonistic and competitive, or good and bad. If we understand cause and condition, we can understand how the welfare of sentient beings rises and falls, how existence begins and ends, and the reality of the universe and of humanity.

Many people misunderstand cause and condition. Three of these common misunderstandings are listed below.

Belief in No Cause and No Condition

There are many people who believe in things like predetermination, random luck, or some sort of divine plan. These perspectives do not look at life from the standpoint of cause and condition. For example, rocks do not normally produce oil, but suppose someone was mining and actually found a rock that has some fossil oil in it. Someone who did not understand cause or condition would not bother analyzing and understanding how this happened, but would consider it a random occurrence.

When a child overeats and chokes to death, instead of thinking they should have prevented the child from overeating, a family that does not understand cause or condition would lament it as destiny. When a botched robbery attempt ends in murder, if the family of the victim does not understand cause and condition, they may simply say it was predetermined. The most pitiful people are those who lay all responsibility at the doorstep of the gods. They deny the value of choice, the meaning of effort, and the importance of self-determination. This total reliance on destiny negates the significance of self-help. It is an erroneous and one-sided view. It is not in accordance with cause and condition.

Belief in Condition, but Not Cause
Many people do not believe in past causes, conditions, and effects.

They believe that life depends on present conditions and current opportunities. They look at mishaps as the lack of proper conditions, or as uncontrollable predicaments. Some siblings in a family persevere and become successful. Others just give up and fail. They blame it all on the lack of opportunities or ill fate and overlook their differences in education and character. Students in the same class finish with different grades. They attribute the differences only to the apparent condition of how much they apply themselves and overlook the underlying causes of the differences in aptitude and intellect. This is only a partial and biased understanding of cause and condition.

Belief in Cause, but Not Condition
Many people look at cause and condition separately. They attribute their circumstances to causes but not to conditions. They overlook the wondrous and dynamic interplay of cause and condition. There are many examples of talented people who fail to live up to their potential, precisely due to the lack of proper conditions in which to exert themselves. When first entering the workforce, they apply for jobs

that call for experienced workers. Finally when they are mature, they only find openings for new graduates. Such situations happen all the time.

Some people view cause and condition as separate and independent. Sometimes they believe in cause but not in condition. Other times, they only accept the existence of condition. These people fail to realize that cause and condition are not static, but are forever changing. They do not stand still or wait for anyone. There is an old saying which illustrates this point, "Good begets blessings; evil will be punished. It is not that there are no effects due to our acts; it is just a matter of time."

The Buddhist View of Cause and Condition

The three views described above are biased and do not reflect the correct understanding of cause and condition. In Buddhism, we believe that cause, condition, reward, and punishment are all intertwined, one giving rise to the other. All things happen due to causes and conditions.

In Buddhism, the common thread for all Dharma is the law

of cause and condition. This is true regardless of the Buddhist school, or whether the Dharma is being viewed on the level of appearance or essence, or whether it is viewed in a worldly or transcendent fashion. All phenomena are products of the proper mix of causes and conditions. It is written in the *Explanation of the Surangama Sutra*, "All holy teachings, from elementary to profound, cannot depart from the law of cause and condition."

It is like building a house. We need bricks, wood, cement, and other materials. The construction can only be completed when one has all the essential materials and all pre-requisites are met. For example, if we want to throw a party, there are many conditions to consider. Do we know our guests well? Can they come? Can we find the appropriate accommodations? Only when all the proper causes and conditions are present can the party be a success. If not, the party will be a flop.

Once, a rich man threw a party. When half of the guests had already arrived, the chef asked if he could start to serve. The man told him to wait a little bit longer. After waiting a few hours, many important guests still had not arrived. Impatient and irritated, the host complained carelessly, "It's not easy throwing a party. The people who shouldn't have come are here, and the people who should be here aren't!"

His seated guests were shocked. They thought to themselves, "I guess I am not really invited. If I am not welcome, I may as well go home."

One by one, the guests quietly slipped away. Seeing the party was dying, the rich man made another careless remark, "It's not easy throwing a party. The people who shouldn't have left are all gone, and the people who should leave are still here!"

After hearing these thoughtless words, every guest was upset. They all stood up and left the party in a huff.

With the appropriate causes and conditions, all endeavors will become successful. If we destroy our own causes and conditions or if we cannot seize the moment available to us due to our own causes and conditions, success will be hard to come by.

CAUSE AND CONDITION AND HUMAN RELATIONSHIPS

These days it is in vogue to talk about "networking." With good interpersonal relationships, everything goes smoothly; otherwise, obstacles and problems abound. Events are the products of combinations, with causes being the major forces and conditions being the minor forces. Interpersonal relationships are a form of cause and condition.

If we want to have a successful business, we must acquire sufficient capital, research the market, and then establish investments. If we do our homework, our businesses will thrive; otherwise, they will fail. Planning and setting up suitable business arrangements are the causes and conditions of business.

We must learn to be humble and be appreciative of the relationships we have with others. Arrogance shuts off even the best of causes and conditions. One such example is the meeting between Bodhidharma and Emperor Wu of the Liang dynasty.

Master Bodhidharma, the First Patriarch of the Chan School, arrived from India in Guangzhou, China by sea during the reign of

Emperor Wu of the Liang dynasty. The emperor quickly sent envoys to accompany Bodhidharma to the capital. Emperor Wu, who wished to show off his past accomplishments, proudly asked Bodhidharma, "I have built temples, sponsored monastics, practiced generosity, and made food offerings. How much merit do you think I have accumulated?"

Dampening the emperor's enthusiasm, Bodhidharma replied coolly, "None at all."

The emperor was very upset. He asked further, "What do you mean? I have done so many good and outstanding acts of benevolence."

Bodhidharma replied, "Your Majesty, those are imperfect causes and will only bring you minor rewards in the human and heavenly realms. They are as illusory as shadows. They are empty phenomena."

"Well, what then is real merit?"

"Do not become attached to the name and form of merit," smiled Bodhidharma. "Purify your thoughts. Realize the ultimate nature of emptiness. Abstain from greed and do not pursue worldly rewards."

The emperor could not understand these profound words. To show off his wisdom as the emperor of his people, he asked in his usual arrogant tone, "Between heaven and earth, who is the holiest?"

Bodhidharma saw through the vanity of the emperor. Not letting up, he replied, "Between heaven and earth, there are neither sages nor ordinary people."

Emperor Wu asked loudly, "Do you know who I am?"

Bodhidharma smiled lightly, shook his head and said, "I do not know."

The emperor always considered himself a great benefactor of Buddhism. He was conceited and not truly sincere about learning the

Truth. How could he possibly take such slighting by Bodhidharma? He immediately flaunted his powers as the emperor and rudely sent Bodhidharma away. In so doing, he lost the cause and condition to learn Chan from Bodhidharma. He dismissed an excellent opportunity to transform Chinese Buddhism. Although he eventually regretted his behavior and tried to send for Bodhidharma again, it was already too late.

As the emperor was egotistical and hungry for fame, he became caught up in the name of merit and strayed from the Middle Way. He could not realize the ultimate truth that is "beyond true or false, beyond good or bad." Since the cause was improper and conditions were poor, the encounter went nowhere.

It is written in the *Flower Adornment Sutra*, "All the waters in the oceans can be consumed, all thoughts as innumerable as specks of dust can be counted, all space can be measured, and all the winds can be stopped; yet, the state of the Buddha can never be fully described." One can further understand cause and condition with this story about Master Huineng, the Sixth Patriarch of the Chan School.

When Huineng was young, he traveled thirty days from Guangdong to Hubei to learn the Dharma from the Fifth Patriarch. When they first met, the Fifth Patriarch immediately knew that Huineng had great potential and that the right causes and conditions were ripening. He asked, "Where are you from? What do you seek?"

"I am a commoner from Xinzhou in Lingnan. I have traveled far to pay homage to you. I seek to be a Buddha and nothing else."

Hearing such a reply, the Fifth Patriarch was impressed. He wanted to test if Huineng had cultivated the right conditions and asked him pointedly, "You are from Lingnan and also a barbarian! How do you expect to be a Buddha?"

Huineng replied calmly and confidently, "Though people may be northerners or southerners, Buddha nature has no north or south. While this barbarian's body is different from yours, Venerable Master, what difference is there in Buddha nature?"

Huineng struck a chord with the Fifth Patriarch. He reflected and replied, "The roots of this barbarian's nature are finely honed. Say no more and go work in the mill!"

Every day for the next eight months, Huineng used a huge axe to collect firewood. Every day, he wore stone weights around his waist to act as ballasts in helping him thresh grains. Not once did the Fifth Patriarch visit him; not once did the Fifth Patriarch teach him one word. Huineng did not complain or get upset. It was late one night when the Fifth Patriarch finally handed Huineng his robe and bowl, making him the Sixth Patriarch. The Fifth Patriarch explained himself with this verse:

Sentient beings come to plant
    seeds,
With them as a cause, they
    ripen.
Without sentience, there are
    no seeds,
Without such nature, there is
    no arising.

What the Fifth Patriarch was saying through this verse is this: When
you first arrived from the distant
land of Lingnan to learn the truth
from me, the cause was ripe and
you were sincere. The environment
and conditions, however, were inadequate. I first needed you to polish

and cultivate yourself for a period of time. Only when the right causes and conditions were met, would I then transmit the teachings.

From this story, we can see how causes and conditions can greatly influence how people interact with one another. Without the appropriate causes and conditions, human relationships will be imperfect and regretful. For things to go as planned, they must wait for the proper causes and conditions to mature. It is like planting flowers. Some seeds planted in spring may blossom in the autumn. Others may take a year to bloom. Some varieties may take even a few years to flower and bear fruit.

Han Yu, a famous Chinese scholar of the Tang dynasty, was demoted and transferred to the remote area of Zhaozhou. As this area was far removed and culturally backward, there were few learned scholars with whom he could converse. When he heard Chan Master Dadian was preaching in the area, he immediately went over for a visit. It just happened that the Chan master was meditating, so Han Yu decided to wait outside.

After a long wait, as the master was still in meditation, Han Yu became restless so he stood up and was about to leave. The master's attendant suddenly said, "First, influence through meditative concentration, then eradicate [arrogance] with wisdom." The words resonated like strong spring thunder and awakened Han Yu. Because his conditions of timing and opportunity were just right at that moment, Han Yu was able and ready to recognize the teaching and learn the way to liberation from the attendant.

Several years ago, a female university graduate left Taiwan with high hopes and traveled halfway across the world to study for her doctorate degree in the United States. After a period of two years in the States, she felt that life was empty and aimless so she packed her bags and returned to Taiwan. From Taipei, she took a two-hour train ride to Hsinchu and became a Buddhist nun.

This news story received a lot of attention when reported by the media. The famous Professor Liang Shiqiu sighed, "If what she had wanted originally was to renounce and become a nun, all she had to do was take a two-hour train ride from Taipei to Hsinchu. There was no need to fly to America. Why spend all that time struggling and then choose to renounce?"

For many of us, the causes and conditions of our lives unfold in a similar way to that woman's decision to renounce and become a nun. Events may come and go, people may meet and separate; however random it may appear, there is meaning in all turns of events. There is an old Chinese saying that captures this well: "Without a bone-chilling freeze, how could plum blossoms have such great fragrance?"

Everything must first have the right causes and proper conditions before results are produced and other favorable conditions are generated. There is the story of Chan Master Shitou Xiqian and his master, Qingyuan Xingsi. When they first met, Qingyuan asked Shitou if he was a student of the Sixth Patriarch, and if he still had any questions, "What did you take with you when you first went to Caoxi?"

"My nature was complete," Shitou smiled. "I was not missing anything prior to studying with the Sixth Patriarch in Caoxi."

"If everything was perfect, why then did you bother to go to study in Caoxi?"

Shitou Xiqian replied definitively, "If I had not gone, how would I have known that I was not lacking in anything? How could I have seen my intrinsic nature?"

All causes and conditions are within us. We must realize the truth in daily life. The continual flow of pure refreshing water is a form of cause and condition. The blossoming of beautiful flowers everywhere is another form of cause and condition. Parents who raise us are our causes and conditions in family relationships. Teachers who educate us are our causes and conditions in the pursuit of knowledge.

Farmers, workers, and merchants who supply our daily needs are the causes and conditions of living in this society. Drivers who transport us here and there are the causes and conditions of traveling. Turning on the television and watching television programs are the causes and conditions of entertainment. It is with these wondrous combinations of causes and conditions that we can live happily and freely.

Regarding the causes and conditions of human relationships, I will cite a verse that can usually be found in temples next to statues of Maitreya Bodhisattva:

Before our eyes are people
connected to us through
conditions;
As we meet and befriend each
other, how can we not be
filled with joy?
The world is full of difficult
and unbearable problems;
As we reap what we sow, why
not open the mind and be
magnanimous?

HOW DO WE KNOW CAUSE AND CONDITION EXIST?

How can we be certain that cause
and condition really exist? How can

it be discovered and understood? For example, suppose a machine in a factory suddenly stops functioning. The technician opens up the machine and discovers a small screw is broken. This small screw is the cause. When cause and condition are not fully satisfied, the machine will not function. When we build a house, if a supporting beam is missing, the roof will collapse. When any ingredient of cause or condition is missing, it can have a great impact on the circumstances of our lives.

Buddhism teaches that our bodies are made up of the combination of the four great elements of earth, water, fire, and wind. These four great elements are the causes. We fall ill when the four elements are not harmonized. Why does a flower fail to blossom? Why is there a poor harvest? It could be a lack of proper conditions, such as inadequate irrigation or fertilizer. Even the space shuttle can be delayed by a simple computer problem. With the slightest offset in cause and condition, the resulting circumstance will be totally different.

No matter what problems or difficulties we face, we must first reflect. We should examine the situation closely for any missing causes and conditions. We should not simply blame the gods or other people, or else we are creating further troubles for ourselves.

Consider a couple who falls in love, only to find that the families oppose the marriage, criticizing the other party as unsuitable, poor, or worse. When these negative conditions, or secondary causes, are absent, the marriage will not work. Other couples fall in love at first sight and get married with lightning speed. The rapid development of events is even beyond their comprehension. The man may say something like, "In my eyes you are a perfect beauty," and the woman may say, "When there is a connection, you can come together across thousands of miles." This is what we call ripened conditions.

I will relate another story to illustrate the existence of cause and condition. Once, King Milinda asked the monk Nagasena, "Are your eyes the real you?"

Nagasena replied, "No."

King Milinda further inquired, "What about the ears?"

"No."

"Does the nose represent you?"

"No."

"Does the tongue represent you?"

"No."

"Then, does it mean that your body is the real you?"

"No, the existence of the body is only a temporary combination of phenomena."

"The mind must be the real you then."

"It is not either."

King Milinda was annoyed and asked further, "Well, if the eyes, ears, nose, tongue, body, and thoughts are not you, then tell me, where is your true self?"

Nagasena grinned and replied

with a question, "Does the window represent the house?"

The king was taken by surprise and struggled for an answer, "No."

"How about the door?"

"No."

"Do the bricks and tiles represent the house?"

"No."

"Then, what about the furniture and pillars?"

"No, of course not."

Nagasena smiled and asked, "If the window, door, bricks, tiles, furniture, and pillars do not represent the house, then where is the real house?"

King Milinda finally understood that causes, conditions, and effects cannot be separated nor understood through a biased and partial view. A house can only be built with the fulfillment of many conditions. Likewise, human existence also needs the satisfaction of many conditions. If we know the law of cause and condition, believe in its existence, plant good causes, and cultivate advantageous conditions, life will be a smooth, successful path.

THE DIFFERENT LEVELS OF CAUSE AND CONDITION

How many varieties of causes and conditions are there? We can examine this from four different perspectives:

Having or Not Having

Causes and conditions are not a matter of knowledge. It cannot be learned by research or via debate. It must be experienced through the heart and mind amidst daily life. If we come to understand cause and condition from real practice and experience, then it can be said that we truly "have" our understanding of cause and condition. According to cause and condition, we are all equal by nature. The universe is us and we are the universe. If we comprehend the law of cause and condition superficially through intellectual speculation or as mere word expressions, then we do not have a true understanding of cause and condition. The result will be as futile as looking for fish in trees.

Bright or Dim

Understanding of cause and condition can be wholesome or unwholesome. Wholesome understanding is

bright, while unwholesome understanding is dim. Suppose a man
lives to be a hundred years old. If
he does not understand birth and
death, if he is not able to clearly see
the reason behind existence, and
only comprehends cause and condition superficially, then he will be
imprisoned by the changed world,
and trapped in his dim understanding of cause and condition, without
a chance at liberation. On the other
hand, if a person has a firm belief
and correct understanding, then his
understanding of cause and condition is bright and virtuous.

Internal or External

Causes and conditions can be understood as internal or external. External causes and conditions are the commonly noticed environmental factors. Internal causes and conditions are more related to intrinsic value. It is like farming a field. The external factors like weather and the environment may be the same, but the harvest from different seeds will vary. Seeds each have different causes and conditions of value. For example, consider how the siblings of the same parents have different temperaments, and the students of the same teacher have varying abilities. External causes and conditions such as parents and teachers may be the same, but the internal causes and conditions of value such as talent and aptitude are very much dissimilar. Therefore, we say that cause and condition may be external and internal. Although external conditions may be complete, if internal causes are inadequate, the resulting effects will leave much to be desired.

Right or Wrong

Our understanding of causes and conditions can also simply be right or wrong. Some people, when they become ill, know that illness is caused by disorders in the body or mind. They are willing to undergo treatment so they can be cured. This is the right understanding of cause and condition. In contrast, there are some people who, when sick, are confused about the true reason for their malady. They are suspicious and attribute their sickness to divine punishment. They go about looking for magical charms, special spells, or they ingest incense ashes. These people only get sicker. This is the wrong understanding of cause and condition. Life may be smooth or bumpy, and obstacles may be many or few. Many of life's difficulties are rooted in misconceptions about the law of cause and condition. We must know how to apply the right understanding and shun wrong views.

HOW TO CREATE WHOLESOME CONDITIONS

Some people say that the greatest invention of the twentieth century is human communication. It is also written in the sutras, "Before becoming Buddhas, we must first cultivate positive conditions with others." To cultivate favorable conditions is to build harmonious relationships and to establish good communication with other people.

One of the greatest treasures of life is "cultivating positive conditions." Building plenty of good conditions is essential for one's happiness in particular and the welfare of the public in general. How, then, can we establish a multitude of good conditions with others?

To cultivate positive conditions with others, people in the past put up lanterns by the side of the road. They built rest stops and provided free tea. They built bridges to establish good conditions with people of the other shore. They dug wells to develop good conditions with everyone. Others may give you a watch or a clock to foster good conditions with you. All of these are examples of building precious good conditions with others. If you have a heart of gold, good conditions will open up everywhere. I can provide you some suggestions on a few methods to form positive conditions with others.

1. *Provide Monetary Assistance*
   We can donate money as a way to build good conditions with others. Not only does it make others feel our concern

for them, it may even save a
life. For example, if there is a
car accident on the road, someone may need a coin to call for
emergency assistance. If you
offer a coin, the person can
make the call. Paramedics and
physicians will then arrive and
provide assistance to the vic-
tims. Your coin will have built
a multitude of good conditions
with others.

2. *Give Kind Encouragement*
When others are frustrated, a
word of encouragement can
bring them immense hope.

When others are disappointed, a word of praise can give them a positive outlook on life. There is a saying that, "A kind word is more valuable than the gift of royal attire; a harsh word is more severe than the fall of the axe." There are times that a few kind words can bring great joy and peace to everyone.

3. *Perform Meritorious Deeds*

A small kind gesture or even a simple kind thought can have tremendous impact. Once upon a time in Holland, there was a child who walked home one evening and saw a small hole in the dike. When he saw that the sea water was slowly seeping in, he thought to himself, "Oh no! How disastrous! If the hole is not patched up immediately, the dam is going to break before dawn and the town will be flooded."

As he could not find anything to patch the hole, he stuck his finger into the hole to stop the leak. He stood like this by the dike throughout the windy rainy night. The whole night passed and not even one person walked by. In the morning, he was found passed out by the dike with his finger still tightly stuck in the hole. The entire town was very grateful to learn that his finger had saved the lives and property of the entire town. Thus there is a saying, "Do not fail to do what is only a little wholesome, do not do what is only a little unwholesome." A simple kind thought can save countless lives and build boundless virtue.

4. *Educate Others*
We can use knowledge and know-how to cultivate favor-

able conditions with others. Each day, there are hundreds of thousands of teachers patiently teaching and passing on their knowledge to the next generation. They are instrumental in promoting the young minds and helping them grow. If you show someone a minor skill, it can be his or her means for future survival. If you teach others a word of wisdom, it can influence his or her entire life and serve as the guiding principle of how he or she deals with others.

5. *Lend a Helping Hand*

We can gain much respect if we accommodate others. The traffic officer helping an elderly person to cross the street becomes a model civil servant. The sales representative who kindly helps shoppers find what they need can make the customers' shopping experience a real pleasure. The young person who politely forfeits his seat to an elderly person gives us confidence in our country's future. By looking at the way we assist others in daily life, we can gauge if we live in a truly progressive and developed society.

6. *Make Warm Gestures*

Sometimes a smile, a nod, or a simple handshake can build unimaginable good conditions. Once in Taiwan, an unemployed young man was wandering the streets near the Taipei train station, wanting to commit suicide by running in front of the car of a wealthy person. In this way, his poor mother would be able to collect some money to live on.

When he was about to make his move, a beautiful gracious lady walked by and smiled at him. He was so excited that he dismissed the idea of committing suicide. The next day, he found a job to support his family. Of course, he no longer wanted to die. Therefore, the smile managed to build great causes and conditions for the young man.

Learning about Buddhism and creating positive conditions is about more than running off to the mountains or donating a lot of money. A kind word, a good deed, a smile, or a bit of know-how can help us build plenty of good conditions and create a great deal of positive karma.

In China, there are four famous mountains. Each of these mountains is associated with a particular bodhisattva. These four bodhisattvas are Avalokitesvara, Ksitigarbha, Manjusri, and Samantabhadra. Each of these bodhisattvas provides us with certain special causes and conditions.

Avalokitesvara   Bodhisattva provides the condition of his loving-kindness and compassion. The bodhisattva brings universal libera-

tion to all. Through the bodhisattva's kind heart and compassionate
vows, all sentient beings may benefit from the Dharma and give rise
to compassion.

Ksitigarbha Bodhisattva provides
the condition of his great vow. The
bodhisattva has vowed to liberate
all sentient beings, and famously
said, "Not until hell is vacant shall
I become a Buddha; only when all
sentient beings are liberated will I
attain awakening." For thousands
of years, Ksitigarbha Bodhisattva's
limitless vow, as reflected in this
verse, has directed countless beings
towards Buddhahood. His vow has

lit an eternal light for the Buddhist teachings.

Manjusri Bodhisattva provides the condition of his wisdom. The bodhisattva uses his extraordinary eloquence to expound the ultimate teachings. He brings light to the blind and the sound of the Dharma to the ignorant. With great wisdom the bodhisattva has propelled Buddhism into the profound and wondrous realm of great *prajna*. Buddhism in China has greatly benefited.

Samantabhadra Bodhisattva provides us the condition of his practice. The bodhisattva shows us the Way with every movement of his hands and feet. With the rising of his eyebrows or the twinkle of his eyes, the bodhisattva expresses the wondrous teachings. In Chinese Buddhism, Samantabhadra Bodhisattva is an exemplary model and has established virtuous ways for cultivating simplicity and striving for thoroughness.

In addition to these four great bodhisattvas, there are countless patriarchs, masters, and Buddhist practitioners who cultivate favorable conditions with others in their unique ways.

Through his calligraphy and by upholding the precepts, Master Hongyi cultivated favorable conditions with others. For those sincerely interested in Buddhism, he often used calligraphy to present the words of Dharma wisdom as the means for cultivating good conditions with them. Personally he was diligent in his cultivation, and he strictly upheld the precepts. He never uttered a word to slight the Dharma nor committed an act in violation of the precepts. His example was like the flowering branches in spring, or the perfect full moon in the sky.

With his meditative concentration, Master Xuyun fostered wholesome conditions with others. He could not be moved by external things, for he was in accord with reality just as it is. His mind was focused and imperturbable. He spread the Dharma without speaking about the teachings. He interacted with different types of people, yet remained true to himself.

Through teaching the Dharma, Master Taixu was able to cultivate favorable conditions with people. He used words to expound the great wisdom of *prajna*. He taught the sutras to awaken the deluded.

He traveled to all corners of China and helped to revive the declining Chinese Buddhism with a dose of effective medicine.

Master Shandao cultivated favorable conditions with others through his light. For those who were physically blind, he ensured that they were not blind in their minds. For those blind in the mind, he brought to them the light of wisdom. He brightened the dark and defiled human existence with his light.

Master Yinguang cultivated favorable connections with others through chanting. With each thought, he was continuously mindful of Amitabha Buddha, and he recited the name of Amitabha Buddha every moment of every day. In this way, he guided the faithful to maintain a strong belief in the Western Pure Land and to form wondrous causes and conditions with Amitabha Buddha.

Other examples include Elder Sudatta in India who gave alms to cultivate favorable conditions with others. He was well respected for building the Jetavana Monastery, which became the center of the Buddha's dispensation in Northern India. Chan Master Yongming

Yanshou cultivated favorable conditions by setting captured animals free. He saved countless animals and marine life from the pain of the slaughterhouse and the torture of the fiery stove in the kitchen. Master Longku used the tea ceremony to cultivate favorable conditions with others. He helped to quench the thirst of exhausted travelers and gave them renewed energy to continue on their long journeys.

Society needs the unity of group effort to thrive, just as the happiness of individual existence relies on the integration of the six senses. Our daily subsistence depends on the close cooperation of all professions working together to facilitate the workings of supply and demand. In this way, we can live in abundance. We should be thankful for the workings of causes and conditions and for the help of all in society.

If we want to be successful and happy, we must cultivate favorable causes and conditions with all beings. We must do it for the present as well as for the future. We should also cultivate favorable Dharma conditions with the Buddhas and bodhisattvas. We must treasure, build, and live within our causes and conditions.

There is a saying, "What comes from the ten directions, goes to the ten directions, to do the work of the ten directions. Ten thousand contribute, ten thousand give, to cultivate ten thousand positive conditions." If we can do this, we will be able to attain Buddhahood and the wisdom of enlightenment.

IV

TIME AND SPACE

TIME EXPANDS ACROSS THE PAST, present and future. Space encompasses hundreds of realms in the ten directions. Most of us think about time as space as much as we think about breathing: all living beings breathe every moment, yet most are not conscious of this action. Depending on our own circumstances, we each understand time and space differently.

For example, certain insects live for a day and are contented; humans live for upwards of seventy years and are still not satisfied. We all confine ourselves to our own limited slice of time and space. From the Buddhist perspective of the cycle of birth and death, the life span of all sentient beings is limitless. Space is boundless and time is immeasurable.

If we penetrate the ultimate truth of time and space, we can be liberated from space as defined by the four directions of north, east, south, and west, and go beyond time's limits of seconds, minutes, days, and months. We can then realize complete freedom.

TIME AND SPACE IN DIFFERENT REALMS

The term "all living beings" includes not only human beings but also beings in the other five realms of existence: heavenly beings, *asuras*, animals, hungry ghosts, and beings in the hell realms. Depending on what realm one resides in, time and space can appear very differently.

Ksana: the Briefest Moment

Buddhism has a specialized vocabulary to discuss extremely vast and extremely small lengths of time. In Buddhism, a *ksana* is the smallest measurable unit of time. Within the context of how we measure time today, it is approximately one seventy-fifth of a second, so it is extremely brief. A single thought occupies ninety *ksanas*, and within a single *ksana* are nine hundred instances of arising and ceasing.

Even within a *ksana*, change happens rapidly. In any particular moment, we see flowers as red and leaves as green. In reality, they are constantly changing from *ksana* to *ksana*, and in time, they will wilt. Within each *ksana*, they are both growing and wilting.

Take the example of a table: we see it standing firmly. However, if we were to look at it under a high powered microscope, we would see that the internal fiber or structure of the wood is changing, expanding and contracting from *ksana* to *ksana* as it decays. After several years, the table can no longer be used.

Are there any flowers or grass in this world which never wilt? Can there be a table that never breaks down? All phenomena arise from *ksana* to *ksana* and all phenomena cease from *ksana* to *ksana*.

Asamkhya Kalpa: the Great Eon

In Buddhism, a very, very long period of time is called an *asamkhya kalpa*. The duration of an *asamkhya kalpa* is so long that any attempts to describe it in words would be futile. There are two lesser units of time described below that can give us an idea of the vastness of an *asamkhya kalpa*.

There is also a unit of time called a "mustard seed *kalpa*." The length of time of a "mustard seed *kalpa*" is described by the following metaphor:

Imagine if we were to take a huge container measuring ten kilometers on each side and filled it with mustard seeds. Then, every one hundred years, we were to remove one seed. The time it would take to empty the container of all the mustard seeds is the length of a "mustard seed *kalpa*."

Another similar unit of time is called a "boulder *kalpa*," and it can also be described by a metaphor. Imagine if we were to take a huge boulder measuring ten kilometers on each side and rubbed the boulder with a piece of sandpaper once every one hundred years. The time it would take to sand down the boulder to dust is the length of a "boulder *kalpa*."

Within the Buddhist time scale, both the "mustard seed *kalpa*" and the "boulder *kalpa*" are considered minor kalpas. In contrast, an *asamkhya kalpa* is a major *kalpa*. It describes a length of time so vast that it is immeasurable and beyond words.

Life Span of Living Beings

The lives of living beings never remain still. Like bubbles on the surface of water, they arise as suddenly as they disappear, each with a different life span. Human beings typically can live for about one hundred years; some insects are born at dawn and are dead by dusk. To such an insect, one day is the equivalent of one hundred years in human terms. Tortoises, the longest living creatures on earth, can live up to two hundred and fifty years; viruses probably perish in less than three hours.

Although there is a huge difference between three hours and two hundred and fifty years, nevertheless, each existence spans a lifetime. Elephants and dolphins can live to be ninety years old. Cows, horses, monkeys, and dogs generally live for fifteen to twenty years. Rats may live for three to four years. Although flies and mosquitoes can only live for a period of about seven days, this is still a lifetime.

However, in the unlimited extent of time and space, these lengths of time are still quite brief. Why? According to Buddhism, there are beings with far longer life spans than human beings. There are several heavenly realms which exist apart from our human realm. The heavenly realm which is most similar to our own is called the "heaven of the four kings." Beings in this heaven can live up to five hundred heavenly years, or 25,000 human years.

Above that is the "heaven of the thirty-three gods." Beings here can live up to 50,000 human years. Beings in the "Yama heaven" have life spans of around 400,000 human years. Beings in the "Tusita heaven" live for about 1,600,000 human years. Beings in the yet higher "heaven of joyful creation" can live for as long as 6,400,000 human years.

Beyond the heavens of the desire realm are the heavens of form realm. The length of the life span there is beyond our comprehension. Within the heavens of the form realm is the "Paranirmita Vasavartin Heaven." Beings there can live the equivalent of 25,600,000 human years. Such long life spans really stretch our imagination.

Beyond the heavens of the form realm are the formless realms. Beings in this realm can live to 80,000 major *kalpas*. The duration of such a life span is incomprehensible. Regardless of how long these beings live, they are nonetheless still trapped in the cycle of birth and death. They still cannot transcend the boundaries of time and space.

Conversely, in those realms below the human realm, such as Avici Hell, beings suffer tremendously. Their ever-expansive bodies and their ever-conscious minds experience relentless torments. Furthermore, time in the Avici Hell stretches out endlessly. The sufferings from the incessant punishments are beyond description.

The Buddhist sutras tell the story of a hungry ghost waiting for spittle. Once there was a hungry ghost that had been starving for a very long time. Since he had not eaten anything for a long time, his hunger was unbearable. Every day, he painfully yearned for something to eat. Eventually, he spotted a person who was about to spit. He eagerly waited for this person to spit so that he could consume the spittle. He waited and waited. During his wait, he saw a city crumble and be rebuilt seven times. Countless time passed before he finally got the spittle. In the lower realms, where there is no day or night, time stretches out frighteningly long.

The Buddhist View of Space

In Buddhism, the largest unit of space is called a Buddha Land, and the smallest unit of space is called a *suksma*, or dust grain. Despite their differences in names, both terms ultimately describe the "three thousand-fold world system," which is analogous to the endless, immeasurable, unlimited, and unbounded universe.

How big is the universe? The planet Earth on which we live is only a part of the solar system, and our Earth is only 1/1,300,000th the size of the sun. Our galaxy the Milky Way galaxy has hundreds of billions of stars like our sun, and a universe probably has hundreds of millions of galaxies like the Milky Way. Just try to imagine the vast immensity of the universe!

On the other end of the scale, modern physics analyzes atoms into even smaller particles called protons, electrons, or neutrons. A *suksma* is smaller than a neutron.

Consider a strand of ox hair. Even though it is very small, if we examine the tip of the ox hair under a high-powered microscope, we would discover that it is made up of many smaller elements. Similarly, a *suksma* is tens of thousands of times smaller than anything we commonly know. Our little finger may look clean and spotless, yet it actually harbors millions of dust particles and microorganisms. Each eye of a housefly consists of four thousand lenses. Such spatial dimension is so minute that it is undetectable by the naked human eye.

With the help of modern laboratory equipment, technology has provided us with a broad and detailed understanding of time and space. When we learn of these modern interpretations based on scientific research, we realize that the universe is indeed extremely vast and deep.

However, the dimensions offered by these interpretations are nonetheless small and shallow when we consider time and space from the Buddhist perspective. Why? In Buddhism, time and space are immense, without an outer limit, and yet at the same time miniscule, without an inner limit. Time and space are immeasurable and boundless.

TIME AND SPACE IN OUR WORLD

Our daily lives in the vast universe are integrally related to time and space. How successful a person is and how effective one handles one's affairs depend on one's management of interpersonal relationships, one's utilization of time, and one's allocation of space.

Without effective timing, we either move too quickly or too slowly, bringing about the resentment of others. Without proper spatial awareness, we end up either taking up others' space or robbing them of their advantageous locations, thereby annoying them. Thus, time and space have a significant impact on our daily existence.

In today's society, some people never seem to have enough time. For them, every second counts. Then there are others for whom time passes by painfully slow, such that days seem like years. Some people are impoverished and homeless; others possess so much land and so many buildings that they even want to own a piece of the moon. But time is most impartial. The poor do not have a minute less; the rich do not have a second more. It cannot be hoarded even with infinite power and might.

Time is the most able judge, as described in the saying, "A long journey can truly test a horse; the passage of time can reveal one's true character." Right or wrong, hatred or love, success or failure—all these will be revealed in time.

The past, present, and future exist in our everyday lives, whether we think life is over at seventy, or if it only begins at seventy. The lives of living beings gradually flow by. The past is quietly gone and will never return. The present shoots by like an arrow and disappears in a flash. The future, amidst our own hesitancy, slowly draws closer and closer, then suddenly slips by.

Time ages everyone, regardless of whether you are rich or poor, or whether you are weak or strong. Once years have passed, hairs do turn gray. Just as there are times when green mountains are blanketed with snow and frost, there will also be a day when we turn gray. Every year we age. The years of human lives disappear in the midst of

the sounds of New Year's firecrack-
ers.

As Buddhists, we strive to cultivate diligently in order to attain
awakening in infinite time and
space. We need to seize eternity
within an instant and to see the
wondrous reality in every flower,
tree, rock, and pool. We can then
venture into the supreme dharma
realm.

We learn to break through the
confines of time, and we must transcend space as well. Some people
climb a mountain to seize land from
the mountain. Others fill the ocean
to claim land from it. In countless

disputes and lawsuits over real estate properties, the living struggle for space with the living. Sometimes the living even struggle with the dead for space, as when graveyards are reclaimed for the construction of housing.

Not only do people have disputes over land, nations also battle over boundary lines to seize more living space for their people. Almost all the wars in the world are fought over land. There is an old saying: "Ten thousand acres of fertile farm land, but how much can one eat in a day? One thousand mansions, but one can only sleep in an eight-foot space." All of space, as it arises and ceases, ultimately comes from the mind.

I often tell people that "trees may live for a thousand years; glory and sorrow cannot last for more than a hundred." We must learn to let go of our attachments, and let go of illusory form. We must transcend the cycle of birth and death, and in doing so, abandon all suffering and attain happiness.

In our daily lives, there are many examples when time and space are simply unbearable. We are often rendered desperate, painful, and hopeless. Things such as being stood up, failing an examination, giving birth, being sick, not being able to find a bathroom, being in a car accident, awaiting sentencing, couples fighting, or facing farewells and deaths—these can happen to any one of us.

These situations can lead to monstrous arguments and endless disputes: this seat is mine; this item is mine; this parcel of land is mine and you may not use it. You did not have time to talk to me because you were in a hurry; you still missed your flight by two minutes. You were upset about not getting on a ship in time, until you found out that you escaped drowning when the ship sank.

A human life is like a flower, blossoming and wilting within a short period of time, and as illusory as the reflection of the moon in the water. For example, consider coming to a lecture hall to hear a Dharma talk. When the time comes, we will all leave, the lights will be switched off, and all sounds will be stilled.

When the doors are closed, the space that was once occupied by the hundreds and thousands of people will be vacated and returned to a state of silence. Yet the connections we create here today will remain for all time and follow us everywhere. All phenomena in this world may disappear like the faded flowers of yesterday. Only connections made through the Dharma last forever.

LIBERATION FROM TIME AND SPACE

Countless masters in Buddhism have achieved the holy fruits of cultivation. They have neither hatred nor attachment. They are relieved of suffering and ignorance. Liberated from the realm of time and space, they exist in total freedom.

For them, time and space are vastly different from what they are for ordinary people.

Great Buddhist sages, being well cultivated in meditation, can stop the mind and calm the heart. They can venture into the profound, subtle, and wondrous dharma realm. They can break through the boundaries of form and liberate themselves from the constraints of time and space. To them, "the short *ksana* is not brief, and the lengthy *asamkhya kalpa* is not long."

Venerable Master Xuyun, a Chan master in recent history, once retreated to Cuiwei Mountain

in Shengxi Province. While waiting for rice to cook, he decided to
meditate for a short time in a cave
and quickly achieved *samadhi*, an
advanced state of meditative concentration. When he came out of
his meditation, the rice was already
completely rotten. He eventually
realized that he had actually medi-
tated for half a year!

Buddhist sages can escape the
constraints of time and space. Their
pure, true nature fills the universe,
and in every moment they are at
ease. Their Dharma body is omni-
present and always at peace everywhere. They can eat one meal a day

and not feel hungry. They can sleep under a tree and be in bliss.

Chan Master Lanrong abandoned fame and fortune and became a monk. With only the bare necessities, consisting of a pair of shoes and a patched robe made out of rags, he retreated to the mountains to cultivate. His younger sister felt sorry for his impoverished lifestyle and took some food and clothing to the cave which he now called home.

When his sister arrived, he kept his eyes closed, did not utter a word, and continued to sit perfectly still in meditation. His sister grew impa-

tient and upset. Consequently, she
threw the things she had brought
into the cave and left. Thirteen years
went by, and his sister continued to
think of him every day. Unable to
stop worrying about him, the sister paid him another visit. He was
still sitting perfectly stationary, like
a rock in meditation. The clothing
and food she had brought thirteen
years earlier remained in exactly
the same location, never touched,
and completely covered with dust.

Chan Master Gaofeng Miao of
the Yuan dynasty also decided to
retreat to a mountain cave to cultivate. There was originally a lad-

der leading up to the cave entrance. Once he got into the cave, he threw the ladder down and was determined not to leave.

Many people felt sorry for him because he could not wash his clothes, take a bath, trim his hair, shave his beard or have anything good to eat. The living space was so narrow that there was barely any room for him to move around. He did not have anyone to talk to and not a friend visited him.

Yet Chan Master Gaofeng Miao endured the unendurable. He did the impossible. Although he did not have a change of clean clothing, his

Dharma appearance was majestic. Although there was no water for bathing, his heart was pure and untainted. He could not shave his hair and beard, yet all his distress was completely eradicated. He did not have any delicious food to eat, yet he savored the delight of meditation and the endless taste of the Dharma. He had no company, but the flowers and trees of nature were full of vitality. Everything he saw was wisdom; every condition he found was wondrous truth. His joy was indescribable.

The freedom and delight enjoyed by these great sages in their liberated state of time and space cannot be matched in our modern, materialistic society. Nowadays people often only focus on pursuing material satisfaction and sensory pleasures. They neglect the peace and serenity of the mind. In reality, more desire will breed more greed and pain. As a result, people become trapped in the drowning mire of evil and cannot break free.

Many people in this modern age are stressed out at work and depressed by life. When the days become unbearable, they go for a vacation abroad to look for a new form of release. Some who live in

Taiwan may visit Southeast Asia, Japan, or Korea. Others may want to really get away by traveling to Europe, the United States, or South Africa. Their efforts are much like digging for a well when one starts to feel thirsty. This is very poor planning indeed!

Seeking relief by expending effort in this way can never liberate someone completely from time and space. To be truly free, one must cultivate the Buddhist teachings. Buddhist practitioners can attain eternity in an instant; they can realize the endless universe in a grain of sand. Unlimited teachings and the endless universe are in our hearts—Why bother to search for them outside?

Countless Chan masters have had the power to break through time and space. With a single thought, they let go of everything. When free of attachments, they are no longer encumbered by time and space. To illustrate my point, allow me to relate a story.

During the Late Liang dynasty, Chan Master Zhisheng, also known as Chan Master Lingshu, preached in Lingshu Temple, which was located near the present day county of Zhujiang in Guangdong Province. The temple had hundreds of resident monks; however, there was no abbot in charge. Some people then urged Chan Master Zhisheng, "Since we have so many monks in this temple now, you should appoint an abbot."

Chan Master Zhisheng reflected for a moment and replied, "The abbot of this temple has already been born into this world. He is now herding sheep. Let's just be patient."

A few years went by and nothing happened. Others once again urged Chan Master Zhisheng to appoint an abbot. Chan Master Zhisheng nodded, "It will be very soon. Our abbot has already renounced the household life to become a monk. Please be patient for a bit longer."

Many years passed, yet the position remained vacant. Others raised the question again. The aging Chan Master Zhisheng smiled and said, "The causes and conditions are gradually ripening. Our abbot is now traveling and studying Chan under many different masters."

After this exchange, Chan Master Zhisheng remained calm and unperturbed. Twenty-two years passed and Chan Master Zhisheng was becoming old. Everyone was now worried. Once more they raised the issue of appointing an abbot with him.

Chan Master Zhisheng looked up to the sky and smiled. He assured everyone, "Good! Good! Our abbot has finally crossed the Five Mountains Range and is heading this way. We will only have to wait a very short while longer." With this said, he then retreated back to his room to meditate.

More time passed. One day, the old master asked the disciples to clean up the abbot's quarters. The old master even inspected the room himself. A few days later, the big bell was rung. Everyone knew it was the signal that the abbot had finally arrived and that they should put on their formal robes. They were to gather before the entrance to welcome the monastic headmaster. Everyone followed the elderly master and stood outside the entrance. Soon, a monk showed up with his alms bowl. He was Chan Master Yunmen Wenyan, who would later become the founder of the Yunmen School of Chan.

Chan Master Zhisheng asked smilingly, "The office of the abbot has been vacant for several decades now. Why are you so late and why did you wait until today to show up?"

Wenyan respectfully joined his palms and replied, "Everything was determined by previous causes and conditions. The length in time and the distance in space are not important. Am I not finally here?"

Chan Master Zhisheng smiled understandingly. Accompanied by all the disciples, he escorted Wenyan into the main shrine and appointed him as the abbot.

How free are the lives of these Chan masters! How unconstrained they are in time and space! In contrast, modern people feast on gourmet food but are not satisfied. They have fame and fortune but no peace. They sleep on comfortable mattresses but toss and turn all night. They reside in mansions but feel insecure. They fight and struggle every day. They can never experience the wonder of limitless time and space. Is this not truly regrettable?

HOW TO USE TIME AND SPACE

The mind can encompass the entire universe, traversing realms as numerous as all the grains of sand. For those who use their time and space wisely, their own time is as immeasurable as the time of the mind. They can freely journey from the past to the present.

For such a person, all of the universe is their time. Their space is the vast dharma realm, where Buddha nature flows everywhere. For those who do not use time wisely, their time is controlled and constrained by the hands of the clock. To them, an hour is an hour, no more, no less; a minute is a minute, no more, no less. Time is limited.

For one who does not know how to use space wisely, their space is area and distance bound by feet and inches. A kilometer cannot be lengthened; a meter cannot be shortened. It is confined and limited.

A devotee once asked Chan Master Zhaozhou, "How can I use the twelve hours of a day wisely?"

Chan Master Zhaozhou stared at him, "You are bound by the twelve hours of the day. I use my twelve hours appropriately. What kind of time are you talking about?"

The wise know how to use time and space perfectly; they lead free and harmonious lives. Fools are enslaved by time and space and are busy running around all day. The difference between the two is obvious.

There is an old fable called "Marking a Boat to Look for a Sword" which illustrates what happens when one is ignorant of time and space. In the country of Chu, a man was crossing a river on a ferry. In the middle of the river, he accidentally dropped his sword.

Everybody urged him to dive into the water to recover the sword. But he wasn't worried. Instead he leisurely made a mark on the side of the ferry, and spoke confidently, "This is the spot where my sword fell. Later, when the boat stops I'll find this mark and dive down to get my sword. Why worry?"

The ferry kept drifting farther and farther from where the man dropped his sword. Others told him that his plan would not work, but he did not listen.

When the boat finally docked, he found his mark and dove down to look for his word. To his surprise, the sword was nowhere to be found. Of course he could not find the sword—he was searching at the wrong time and in the wrong place.

As we all work in society, some people just want to make a lot of money. They work day and night, scheme and cheat, and use every avenue to make money. They may make ten thousand a month, a hundred thousand a year. Over the course of their lives they may earn a few million dollars.

From this amount, if you deduct the expenses for clothing, meals, and entertainment, how much money is left? To forego all ideals and happiness for a few hundred thousand dollars, what is the meaning of this? What is the value of life? Is it really worthwhile to throw away a precious lifetime in exchange for a few crumpled bills? Why do we not use our valuable time to pursue the path of real fortune and happiness?

When I first arrived in Taiwan in 1949, not only was I unable to replace my old torn clothes and shoes, but I also had great difficulty obtaining a pen and some paper to write with. Sometimes I had to endure hunger and being cold for months and still I could not afford to have these few items. But when I saw others receiving generous offerings through chanting sutras or conducting funeral services I did not feel inadequate. They were able to buy comfortable clothing and good food; I still did not feel poor or deprived.

In cold weather, I warmed myself under the sun. The sun was there for everyone to enjoy. The sun was my robe; it was so very warm. During the hot season, I cooled myself with the breezes. The wind was there to keep everyone cool. The wind was my gown; it was so very freeing. I looked at trees and flowers; they were my Dharma companions. No one could restrict me. I had oh so many Dharma companions. I walked across rivers and plains; they gave me so much Dharma joy.

No one could take that away from me.

If our minds are broad and open, the sky, the land, the sun, and the moon are all ours. We can have all time and space. If all you know is how to complain and get depressed about poverty and obstacles, you will be poor and ill at ease in all places and at all times. All your time and space will become an endless hell and a boundless sea of suffering.

One day, a young person saw a very old man. He was curious and asked, "Sir, can you tell me how old you are?"

With a smile, the gentlemen replied, "Oh! I am four. I am four years old."

The young fellow was shocked. He looked the old gentleman up and down, "Sir, please do not joke with me. Your hair is so white and your beard is so long. How could you be four?"

"Yes! I am really four!" Then the old man kindly explained, "In the past, I lived a befuddled life. I was selfish and preoccupied. I wasted away a great portion of my life. It wasn't until four years ago that I discovered Buddhism. Then I learned to do good and be helpful. I learned to get rid of my greed, hatred, and ignorance. I realized that I should cultivate myself to find my true nature. Until these past four years, my entire life had not been meaningful, valuable, or fulfilling. You asked me my age. I really feel I have been a worthwhile person for only these four years. That is why I am only four."

We should do wholesome deeds sooner rather than later, and we should learn the Dharma as early as possible. In your brief existence in time and space, how have you lived your life? Have you used the opportunity to do good and to seek the truth? Have you used all available time and space to benefit yourself and others?

In the Buddhist sutras there is a story of a king and his two attendants. The king liked his attendant on the left much better than he did the one on the right. The attendant on the right was puzzled and wondered why he was not in the king's favor. He carefully monitored every move of the other attendant and, finally, he discovered the reason.

When the king spit, the attendant on the left would quickly wipe away the spit off the ground with his foot. Naturally, the king liked him better. With this knowledge, the attendant on the right planned to do the same. He was, however, always a bit slower than the other attendant, and would always miss the opportunity to wipe away the king's spit.

Finally, he thought of a plan. The next time the king was ready to spit, he would jump on the opportunity. He figured that if he aimed correctly, he would be able to wipe away the spit from the king's mouth before it could land on the ground. Unfortunately, when he kicked his foot up, he knocked out the king's teeth and bloodied his mouth. In this way, he also "wiped away" any opportunities he had to earn the king's favor.

Greed and ignorance prevent us from using time and space wisely, missing out on valuable opportunities. Only if we want to benefit others and ourselves, can we seize boundless time and space.

Once, a high official in Japan asked Chan Master Zian about the use of time. The official complained, "I have a meaningless job. Every day, people want to flatter me. After a while, all compliments sound the same and are actually quite tedious. I do not enjoy hearing all the flattery. Days seem to pass by like years. I just do not know how to pass the time."

The Chan master smiled and gave him these words, "This day will never return; the passing of time is as precious as treasure." Time once passed will never return. We should treasure our time and remember that time is precious, like exquisite jade.

Nowadays, it is fashionable to talk about "conservation." Unfortunately, we only emphasize conserving materials and money. We do not know that we should also conserve time as well as our emotions. We should conserve our desires and our lives. We should be careful with every thought and deed. We should not let ourselves be indulgent and lose control. Only then can we know how to use time and space wisely.

Chan Master Zongyan of Japan liked to take afternoon naps. It was his habit. His students asked him why he slept so long. He replied, "What do you know? In my dreams, I visit ancient scholars and masters, much like Confucius dreaming of the Duke of Zhou. The longer my dreams are, the better my cultivation is."

One day, a few students were scolded by the same Chan master for taking long afternoon naps. One student replied, "Well. We are learning from your example. In our dreams we have gone to seek out and study with ancient masters and scholars."

"What then have you learned from them?"

"In our dreams, we visited many ancient masters and scholars. We asked them, 'Is our master studying with you all the time?' They all replied, 'No, we have never seen or heard of your master.'"

One must be true and honest about time and space. Day by day, time goes by and will never return. Time never flows backwards. If we do not seize opportunities, we will not be able to make anything out of them.

In Buddhism, the "Take Heed Verse" of Samantabadhra Bodhisattva aptly describes the urgency of using our time wisely:

> This day is done; your life has lessened.
> As a fish in dwindling water, where is the joy?

Practice diligently as if your
    head was on fire.
Be mindful of impermanence;
    do not relax your efforts.

Time and space quickly disappear. If we want to seize time and
space, if we treasure life, we should
chant "Amitofo," the name of Amitabha Buddha. "Amitofo" means
both infinite light and infinite life.
Infinite light is boundless space; infinite life is endless time. If we can
make time and space boundless and
limitless, we will have risen above
the confinement of time and space.
We will have broken away from

the cycle of birth and death. We will have turned ignorance into enlightenment. We will have escaped from the sea of suffering, from the cycle of birth and death, and have transcended the confusion and hindrance of worldly phenomena. We will have ventured into the bright and free world of *nirvana*, the Pure Land of Ultimate Bliss.

ABOUT THE AUTHOR

Venerable Master Hsing Yun is a Chinese Buddhist monk, philanthropist, author, innovator and founder of the Fo Guang Shan Buddhist Order, which has more than 200 temples throughout Taiwan, greater Asia, North and South America, Europe, Africa, and Australia. He is also the founder of Buddha's Light International Association, a worldwide lay service and humanitarian organization with over one million active members. Master Hsing Yun has spent his life as a monk promoting "Humanistic Buddhism":

Buddhism that meets the needs of people and is integrated into all aspects of life.

Master Hsing Yun has written more than one hundred books on how to find happiness, peace, compassion and wisdom through serving others. His writings appear in twenty languages, including numerous and award-winning English-language translations, such as *Being Good*, *For All Living Beings*, and *Pearls of Wisdom*. His broad and deep contributions also include establishing Buddhist art galleries and sponsoring Buddhist music, as well as establishing Buddhist-based educational institutions ranging from kindergartens to universities, most notably the University of the West in Rosemead, California.

Today Master Hsing Yun continues to travel around the world teaching the Dharma. He faithfully writes his daily column for the *Merit Times* and produces Dharma-inspired one-stroke calligraphy paintings. He continues to guide the Buddha's Light International Association as its acting president.

About
Buddha's Light Publishing

Buddha's Light Publishing offers quality translations of classical Buddhist texts as well as works by contemporary Buddhist teachers and scholars. We embrace Humanistic Buddhism, and promote Buddhist writing which is accessible, community-oriented, and relevant to daily life.

Founded in 1996 by Venerable Master Hsing Yun as the Fo Guang Shan International Translation Center, Buddha's Light Publishing seeks to continue Master Hsing

Yun's goal of promoting the Buddha's teachings by fostering writing, art, and culture. Learn more by visiting www.blpusa.com.